BARRON'S

COMMON CORE SUCCESS
LEARN, REVIEW, APPLY

GRADE 6 MATH

Christina Lynn Louis
Consulting Editor

All inquiries should be addressed to:
Barron's Educational Series, Inc.
250 Wireless Boulevard
Hauppauge, NY 11788
www.barronseduc.com

ISBN 978-1-4380-0680-2

Library of Congress Control Number: 2015932218

Date of Manufacture: May 2015
Manufactured by: C&C Offset Printing Co., Ltd, Shenzhen, China

Printed in China

9 8 7 6 5 4 3 2 1

The recent adoption of the Common Core Standards now provides a distinct path to mathematic success. The standards are clear, the performance expectations are high, and the need for problem-solving is rigorous. The transition to this new method has been demanding for teachers, students, and parents alike. As a matter of fact, many parents, tutors, and even older siblings often think, "We never did it this way!"

Charged with the task of creating a parent-friendly mathematics handbook, we realized this was our opportunity to become the support that is critically needed. As classroom teachers for over forty-six years collectively, we have worked collaboratively for a number of years to improve our math instructional practices. Our math instruction evolved as a result of many research projects conducted within our classrooms. Using this research, we developed innovative ways to teach concepts otherwise viewed as extremely difficult by our students. We know what has to be taught, and we understand the struggles that students experience as they strive to achieve mastery.

The new Common Core Standards call for higher-level thinking and in-depth application of math content in multi-step word problems. Along with Common Core content standards, there are eight practice standards that dictate the behaviors required of our students as they engage in mathematics. As a result, we have implemented our Ace It Time! activity, or what Van de Walle refers to as a "math-rich" problem for each lesson. This is a rubric or checklist that will guide each student in the problem-solving process. It will also challenge him or her to explain his or her own thinking. This is often an element missing within most home resources. Parents will be able to turn to our product for support, insight, and assistance. They will have an invaluable resource that explains the standards in parent-friendly language, outlines the task required for that standard, teaches it in an easy-to-understand way, and provides adequate opportunities for practice. You will find that resource in our Barron's Common Core Success Math Series.

Parents, teachers, tutors, and other homework helpers—we wish you much success in your journey to help your student master the Common Core!

Jessica Snyder, M.Ed.
Colleen Oppenzato, B.A.

Introduction to Problem Solving and Mathematical Practices

For parents, tutors, teachers and homework helpers: Problem solving in the mathematics classroom involves more than calculations alone. It involves a student's ability to consistently show his or her reasoning and comprehension skills to model and explain what he or she has been taught. These skills will form the basis for future success in meeting life's goals. Working through the Common Core State Standards each year through the twelfth grade sets the necessary foundation for collegiate and career success. Your student will be better prepared to handle the challenges that await him or her as he or she gradually enters into the global marketplace.

The next few pages contain a listing of the sixth grade Common Core State Standards your student will need to master.

Ratios & Proportional Relationships

Understand ratio concepts and use ratio reasoning to solve problems.

CCSS.MATH.CONTENT.6.RP.A.1 – Understand the concept of a ratio and use ratio language to describe a ratio relationship between two quantities. For example, "The ratio of wings to beaks in the bird house at the zoo was 2:1, because for every 2 wings there was 1 beak." "For every vote candidate A received, candidate C received nearly three votes."

CCSS.MATH.CONTENT.6.RP.A.2 – Understand the concept of a unit rate $\frac{a}{b}$ associated with a ratio a:b with b ≠ 0, and use rate language in the context of a ratio relationship. For example, "This recipe has a ratio of 3 cups of flour to 4 cups of sugar, so there is $\frac{3}{4}$ cup of flour for each cup of sugar." "We paid $75 for 15 hamburgers, which is a rate of $5 per hamburger."

CCSS.MATH.CONTENT.6.RP.A.3 – Use ratio and rate reasoning to solve real-world and mathematical problems, e.g., by reasoning about tables of equivalent ratios, tape diagrams, double number line diagrams, or equations.

CCSS.MATH.CONTENT.6.RP.A.3.A – Make tables of equivalent ratios relating quantities with whole-number measurements, find missing values in the tables, and plot the pairs of values on the coordinate plane. Use tables to compare ratios.

CCSS.MATH.CONTENT.6.RP.A.3.B – Solve unit rate problems including those involving unit pricing and constant speed. For example, if it took 7 hours to mow 4 lawns, then at that rate, how many lawns could be mowed in 35 hours? At what rate were lawns being mowed?

CCSS.MATH.CONTENT.6.RP.A.3.C – Find a percent of a quantity as a rate per 100 (e.g., 30% of a quantity means $\frac{30}{100}$ times the quantity); solve problems involving finding the whole, given a part and the percent.

CCSS.MATH.CONTENT.6.RP.A.3.D – Use ratio reasoning to convert measurement units; manipulate and transform units appropriately when multiplying or dividing quantities.

The Number System

Apply and extend previous understandings of multiplication and division to divide fractions by fractions.

CCSS.MATH.CONTENT.6.NS.A.1 – Interpret and compute quotients of fractions, and solve word problems involving division of fractions by fractions, e.g., by using visual fraction models and equations to represent the problem. For example, create a story context for $(\frac{2}{3}) \div (\frac{3}{4})$ and use a visual fraction model to show the quotient; use the relationship between multiplication and division to explain that $(\frac{2}{3}) \div (\frac{3}{4}) = \frac{8}{9}$ because $\frac{3}{4}$ of $\frac{8}{9}$ is $\frac{2}{3}$. (In general, $(\frac{a}{b}) \div (\frac{c}{d}) = \frac{ad}{bc}$.) How much chocolate will each person get if 3 people share $\frac{1}{2}$ lb of chocolate equally? How many $\frac{3}{4}$-cup servings are in $\frac{2}{3}$ of a cup of yogurt? How wide is a rectangular strip of land with length $\frac{3}{4}$ mi and area $\frac{1}{2}$ square mi?

Compute fluently with multi-digit numbers and find common factors and multiples.

CCSS.MATH.CONTENT.6.NS.B.2 – Fluently divide multi-digit numbers using the standard algorithm.

CCSS.MATH.CONTENT.6.NS.B.3 – Fluently add, subtract, multiply, and divide multi-digit decimals using the standard algorithm for each operation.

CCSS.MATH.CONTENT.6.NS.B.4 – Find the greatest common factor of two whole numbers less than or equal to 100 and the least common multiple of two whole numbers less than or equal to 12. Use the distributive property to express a sum of two whole numbers 1–100 with a common factor as a multiple of a sum of two whole numbers with no common factor. For example, express 36 + 8 as 4 (9 + 2).

Apply and extend previous understandings of numbers to the system of rational numbers.

CCSS.MATH.CONTENT.6.NS.C.5 – Understand that positive and negative numbers are used together to describe quantities having opposite directions or values (e.g., temperature above/below zero, elevation above/below sea level, credits/debits, positive/negative electric charge); use positive and negative numbers to represent quantities in real-world contexts, explaining the meaning of 0 in each situation.

CCSS.MATH.CONTENT.6.NS.C.6 – Understand a rational number as a point on the number line. Extend number line diagrams and coordinate axes familiar from previous grades to represent points on the line and in the plane with negative number coordinates.

CCSS.MATH.CONTENT.6.NS.C.6.A – Recognize opposite signs of numbers as indicating locations on opposite sides of 0 on the number line; recognize that the opposite of the opposite of a number is the number itself, e.g., –(–3) = 3, and that 0 is its own opposite.

CCSS.MATH.CONTENT.6.NS.C.6.B – Understand signs of numbers in ordered pairs as indicating locations in quadrants of the coordinate plane; recognize that when two ordered pairs differ only by signs, the locations of the points are related by reflections across one or both axes.

CCSS.MATH.CONTENT.6.NS.C.6.C – Find and position integers and other rational numbers on a horizontal or vertical number line diagram; find and position pairs of integers and other rational numbers on a coordinate plane.

CCSS.MATH.CONTENT.6.NS.C.7 – Understand ordering and absolute value of rational numbers.

CCSS.MATH.CONTENT.6.NS.C.7.A – Interpret statements of inequality as statements about the relative position of two numbers on a number line diagram. For example, interpret –3 > –7 as a statement that –3 is located to the right of –7 on a number line oriented from left to right.

CCSS.MATH.CONTENT.6.NS.C.7.B – Write, interpret, and explain statements of order for rational numbers in real-world contexts. For example, write –3 °C > –7 °C to express the fact that –3 °C is warmer than –7 °C.

CCSS.MATH.CONTENT.6.NS.C.7.C – Understand the absolute value of a rational number as its distance from 0 on the number line; interpret absolute value as magnitude for a positive or negative quantity in a real-world situation. For example, for an account balance of –30 dollars, write $|-30| = 30$ to describe the size of the debt in dollars.

CCSS.MATH.CONTENT.6.NS.C.7.D – Distinguish comparisons of absolute value from statements about order. For example, recognize that an account balance less than –30 dollars represents a debt greater than 30 dollars.

CCSS.MATH.CONTENT.6.NS.C.8 – Solve real-world and mathematical problems by graphing points in all four quadrants of the coordinate plane. Include use of coordinates and absolute value to find distances between points with the same first coordinate or the same second coordinate.

Expressions and Equations

Apply and extend previous understandings of arithmetic to algebraic expressions.

CCSS.MATH.CONTENT.6.EE.A.1 – Write and evaluate numerical expressions involving whole-number exponents.

CCSS.MATH.CONTENT.6.EE.A.2 – Write, read, and evaluate expressions in which letters stand for numbers.

CCSS.MATH.CONTENT.6.EE.A.2.A – Write expressions that record operations with numbers and with letters standing for numbers. For example, express the calculation "Subtract y from 5" as 5 – y.

CCSS.MATH.CONTENT.6.EE.A.2.B – Identify parts of an expression using mathematical terms (sum, term, product, factor, quotient, coefficient); view one or more parts of an expression as a single entity. For example, describe the expression 2 (8 + 7) as a product of two factors; view (8 + 7) as both a single entity and a sum of two terms.

CCSS.MATH.CONTENT.6.EE.A.2.C – Evaluate expressions at specific values of their variables. Include expressions that arise from formulas used in real-world problems. Perform arithmetic operations, including those involving whole-number exponents, in the conventional order when there are no parentheses to specify a particular order (Order of Operations). For example, use the formulas $V = s^3$ and $A = 6s^2$ to find the volume and surface area of a cube with sides of length $s = \frac{1}{2}$.

CCSS.MATH.CONTENT.6.EE.A.3 – Apply the properties of operations to generate equivalent expressions. For example, apply the distributive property to the expression $3(2 + x)$ to produce the equivalent expression $6 + 3x$; apply the distributive property to the expression $24x + 18y$ to produce the equivalent expression $6(4x + 3y)$; apply properties of operations to $y + y + y$ to produce the equivalent expression $3y$.

CCSS.MATH.CONTENT.6.EE.A.4 – Identify when two expressions are equivalent (i.e., when the two expressions name the same number regardless of which value is substituted into them). For example, the expressions $y + y + y$ and $3y$ are equivalent because they name the same number regardless of which number y stands for.

Reason about and solve one-variable equations and inequalities.

CCSS.MATH.CONTENT.6.EE.B.5 – Understand solving an equation or inequality as a process of answering a question: which values from a specified set, if any, make the equation or inequality true? Use substitution to determine whether a given number in a specified set makes an equation or inequality true.

CCSS.MATH.CONTENT.6.EE.B.6 – Use variables to represent numbers and write expressions when solving a real-world or mathematical problem; understand that a variable can represent an unknown number, or, depending on the purpose at hand, any number in a specified set.

CCSS.MATH.CONTENT.6.EE.B.7 – Solve real-world and mathematical problems by writing and solving equations of the form $x + p = q$ and $px = q$ for cases in which p, q and x are all non-negative rational numbers.

CCSS.MATH.CONTENT.6.EE.B.8 – Write an inequality of the form $x > c$ or $x < c$ to represent a constraint or

condition in a real-world or mathematical problem. Recognize that inequalities of the form $x > c$ or $x < c$ have infinitely many solutions; represent solutions of such inequalities on number line diagrams.

Represent and analyze quantitative relationships between dependent and independent variables.

CCSS.MATH.CONTENT.6.EE.C.9 – Use variables to represent two quantities in a real-world problem that change in relationship to one another; write an equation to express one quantity, thought of as the dependent variable, in terms of the other quantity, thought of as the independent variable. Analyze the relationship between the dependent and independent variables using graphs and tables, and relate these to the equation. For example, in a problem involving motion at constant speed, list and graph ordered pairs of distances and times, and write the equation $d = 65t$ to represent the relationship between distance and time

Geometry

Solve real-world and mathematical problems involving area, surface area, and volume.

CCSS.MATH.CONTENT.6.G.A.1 – Find the area of right triangles, other triangles, special quadrilaterals, and polygons by composing into rectangles or decomposing into triangles and other shapes; apply these techniques in the context of solving real-world and mathematical problems.

CCSS.MATH.CONTENT.6.G.A.2 – Find the volume of a right rectangular prism with fractional edge lengths by packing it with unit cubes of the appropriate unit fraction edge lengths, and show that the volume is the same as would be found by multiplying the edge lengths of the prism. Apply the formulas $V = l\,w\,h$ and $V = b\,h$ to find volumes of right rectangular prisms with fractional edge lengths in the context of solving real-world and mathematical problems.

CCSS.MATH.CONTENT.6.G.A.3 – Draw polygons in the coordinate plane given coordinates for the vertices; use coordinates to find the length of a side joining points with the same first coordinate or the same second coordinate. Apply these techniques in the context of solving real-world and mathematical problems.

CCSS.MATH.CONTENT.6.G.A.4 – Represent three-dimensional figures using nets made up of rect-

angles and triangles, and use the nets to find the surface area of these figures. Apply these techniques in the context of solving real-world and mathematical problems.

Statistics and Probability

Develop understanding of statistical variability.

CCSS.MATH.CONTENT.6.SP.A.1 – Recognize a statistical question as one that anticipates variability in the data related to the question and accounts for it in the answers. For example, "How old am I?" is not a statistical question, but "How old are the students in my school?" is a statistical question because one anticipates variability in students' ages.

CCSS.MATH.CONTENT.6.SP.A.2 – Understand that a set of data collected to answer a statistical question has a distribution which can be described by its center, spread, and overall shape.

CCSS.MATH.CONTENT.6.SP.A.3 – Recognize that a measure of center for a numerical data set summarizes all of its values with a single number, while a measure of variation describes how its values vary with a single number.

Summarize and Describe Distributions

CCSS.MATH.CONTENT.6.SP.B.4 – Display numerical data in plots on a number line, including dot plots, histograms, and box plots.

CCSS.MATH.CONTENT.6.SP.B.5 – Summarize numerical data sets in relation to their context, such as by:

CCSS.MATH.CONTENT.6.SP.B.5.A – Reporting the number of observations.

CCSS.MATH.CONTENT.6.SP.B.5.B – Describing the nature of the attribute under investigation, including how it was measured and its units of measurement.

CCSS.MATH.CONTENT.6.SP.B.5.C – Giving quantitative measures of center (median and/or mean) and variability (interquartile range and/or mean absolute deviation), as well as describing any overall pattern and any striking deviations from the overall pattern with reference to the context in which the data were gathered.

CCSS.MATH.CONTENT.6.SP.B.5.D – Relating the choice of measures of center and variability to the shape of the data distribution and the context in which the data were gathered.

Making Sense of the Problem-Solving Process

For students: The eight mathematical practices outlined in the Common Core State Standards ask you to make sense of word problems, write word problems with numbers and symbols, and be able to prove when you are right as well as to know when a mistake happened. These eight practices also state that you may solve a problem by drawing a model, using a chart, list, or other tool. When you get your correct answer, you must be able to explain how and why you chose to solve it that way. Every word problem in this workbook addresses at least three of these practices, helping to prepare you for the demands of problem solving in your sixth grade classroom. The first unit of this book discusses the **Ace It Time!** section of each lesson. **Ace It Time!** will help you master these practices.

While Doing Mathematics You Will...

1. Make sense of problems and become a champion in solving them

- Solve problems and discuss how you solved them
- Look for a starting point and plan to solve the problem
- Make sense (meaning) of a problem and search for solutions

- Use concrete objects or pictures to solve problems
- Check over work by asking, "Does this make sense?"
- Plan out a problem-solving approach

2. Reason on concepts and understand that they are measurable

- Understand numbers represent specific quantities
- Connect quantities to written symbols
- Take a word problem and represent it with numbers and symbols

- Know and use different properties of operations
- Connect addition and subtraction to length

3. Construct productive arguments and compare the reasoning of others

- Construct arguments using concrete objects, pictures, drawings and actions
- Practice having conversations/discussions about math
- Explain your own thinking to others and respond to the thinking of others

- Ask questions to clarify the thinking of others (How did you get that answer? Why is that true?)
- Justify your answer and determine if the thinking of others is correct

4. Model with mathematics

- Determine ways to represent the problem mathematically
- Represent story problems in different ways; examples may include numbers, words, drawing pictures, using objects, acting out, making a chart or list, writing equations

- Find opportunities to make connections between the previous representations and explain
- Evaluate your answers and think about whether or not they make sense

5. Use appropriate tools strategically

- Consider available tools when solving math problems
- Choose tools appropriately

- Determine when certain tools might be helpful
- Use technology to help with understanding

6. Attend to detail

- Develop math communication skills by using clear and exact language in your math conversations

- Understand meanings of symbols and label appropriately
- Calculate accurately

7. Look for and make use of structure

- Apply general math rules to specific situations
- Look for patterns or structure to help solve problems

- Adopt mental math strategies based on patterns such as making ten, fact families, and doubles

8. Look for and express regularity in repeated reasoning

- Notice repeated calculations and look for shortcut methods to solve problems (for example, rounding up and adjusting the answer to compensate for the rounding)

- Evaluate your own work by asking, "Does this make sense?"

For the official Standards of Mathematical Practice, please visit www.corestandards.org/Math/Practice.

9

Contents

UNPACK THE STANDARD
You will make sense of word problems and use strategies to solve them.

LEARN IT: You are about to learn a lot of different math strategies. This book will help you master multiplication, division, and fractions. Before starting, let's review some strategies that work for all types of problems. You will use these tricks in the Ace It Time! section in each lesson.

STEP 1: UNDERSTAND
What's the Question?

Math problems can have many steps. Each of the steps is shown on the checklist.

The first step is to read the problem and ask yourself, "What question do I have to answer?" and "Will it take more than one step to solve the problem?"

When you find the question, underline it. Then check "Yes" on the checklist.

Practice: Underline the question.

Simonne wants to buy a video game. The game costs $144. She already has $88 saved. Her plan is to save seven dollars a month until she has enough money to buy the game. <u>How many months will it take Simonne to save enough money to buy her video game?</u>

Will it take more than one step to solve the problem? Yes.

ACE IT TIME!

	yes	no
Did you underline the question in the word problem?	yes ○	no ○
Did you circle the numbers or number words?	yes ○	no ○
Did you box the supporting details or information needed to solve the problem?	yes ○	no ○
Did you draw a picture or a graphic organizer and write a math sentence to show your thinking?	yes ○	no ○
Did you label your numbers and your picture?	yes ○	no ○
Did you explain your thinking and use math vocabulary words in your explanation?	yes ○	no ○

STEP 2: IDENTIFY
What Numbers or Words are needed?

It is very important to locate the numbers you will use to solve the problem. When you find the numbers, circle them. Then check "Yes" on the checklist. *Remember:* Numbers can be written in number form or in word form.

Practice: Circle the numbers you need to solve the problem.

Example: Simonne wants to buy a video game. The game costs $144. She already has $88 saved. Her plan is to save seven dollars a month until she has enough money to buy the game. How many months will it take Simonne to save enough money to buy her video game?

ACE IT TIME!

	yes	no
Did you underline the question in the word problem?	○	○
Did you circle the numbers or number words?	○	○
Did you box the supporting details or information needed to solve the problem?	○	○
Did you draw a picture or a graphic organizer and write a math sentence to show your thinking?	○	○
Did you label your numbers and your picture?	○	○
Did you explain your thinking and use math vocabulary words in your explanation?	○	○

STEP 3: RECOGNIZE THE SUPPORTING DETAILS
Name the Operation

In every problem, there will be clues that help you figure out if you are adding, subtracting, multiplying, or dividing. Put a box around the clues. Then check "Yes" on the checklist.

Practice: Put a box around the clues.

Example: Simonne wants to buy a video game. The game costs $144. She already has $88 saved. Her plan is to save seven dollars a month until she has enough money to buy the game. How many months will it take Simonne to save enough money to buy her video game?

This is a two-step problem. You will first subtract what she has already saved from the total cost of the game to figure out how much more she will need. After you figure out how much more money she needs, you will divide that amount by the seven dollars a month that she plans to save. This will tell you how many months she needs to save.

STEPS 4–5: SOLVE AND LABEL

It is important that you connect words in your problem to pictures and numbers. Before solving, you should draw a picture or write a math equation

ACE IT TIME!

	yes	no
Did you underline the question in the word problem?		
Did you circle the numbers or number words?		
Did you box the supporting details or information needed to solve the problem?		
Did you draw a picture or a graphic organizer and write a math sentence to show your thinking?		
Did you label your numbers and your picture?		
Did you explain your thinking and use math vocabulary words in your explanation?		

ACE IT TIME!

	yes	no
Did you underline the question in the word problem?		
Did you circle the numbers or number words?		
Did you box the supporting details or information needed to solve the problem?		
Did you draw a picture or a graphic organizer and write a math sentence to show your thinking?		
Did you label your numbers and your picture?		
Did you explain your thinking and use math vocabulary words in your explanation?		

 Standards: CCSS.Math.Practice.MP1, MP2, MP3, MP4, MP5, MP6, MP7, MP8, CCSS.Math.Content.6.NS.B.2

to solve the problem. Make sure to label your pictures and equations. Then check "Yes" on the checklist.

Let's Practice:

Step 1:

Subtract 88 from 144. I can use a number line and count backwards from 144 until I get to 88.

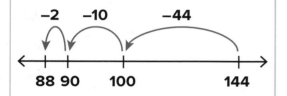

−2   −10   −44

88 90   100   144

I know that 44 + 10 + 2 = 56

So . . . 144 − 88 = 56.
She needs to save $56 more.

Step 2:

quotient
(number of months needed to save money)

56 ÷ 7 = 8

divisor
(money saved per month)

dividend
(money still needed to buy game)

So, $56 ÷ $7 each month equals 8 months of saving.

ACE IT TIME!

	yes	no
Did you underline the question in the word problem?	○	○
Did you circle the numbers or number words?	○	○
Did you box the supporting details or information needed to solve the problem?	○	○
Did you draw a picture or a graphic organizer and write a math sentence to show your thinking?	○	○
Did you label your numbers and your picture?	○	○
Did you explain your thinking and use math vocabulary words in your explanation?	○	○

STEP 6: EXPLAIN

Write a Response. Use Math Vocabulary.

You are almost done! Explain your answer and show your thinking. Write in complete sentences to explain the steps you used to solve the problem. Use the vocabulary words in the Math Vocabulary box to help you.

Example: Simonne wants to buy a video game. The game costs $144. She already has $88 saved. Her plan is to save seven dollars a month until she has enough money to buy the game. How many months will it take Simonne to save enough money to buy her video game?

Explanation: First, I found out how much money she needs to get the video game by subtracting how much money she already has saved from the total cost of the game (144 − 88 = 56.) Next, I found out how many months it will take Simonne to save for the game by using division to solve 56 ÷ 7, because she plans to save $7 each month. So I **divided** my **dividend** (56) by my **divisor** (7). This gave me my **quotient** of 8 months that Simonne needs to save in order to get her video game.

ACE IT TIME!

	yes	no
Did you underline the question in the word problem?	○	○
Did you circle the numbers or number words?	○	○
Did you box the supporting details or information needed to solve the problem?	○	○
Did you draw a picture or a graphic organizer and write a math sentence to show your thinking?	○	○
Did you label your numbers and your picture?	○	○
Did you explain your thinking and use math vocabulary words in your explanation?	○	○

Math Vocabulary

divide

dividend

divisor

quotient

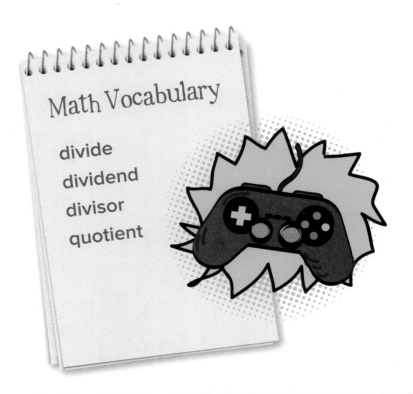

Standards: CCSS.Math.Practice.MP1, MP2, MP3, MP4, MP5, MP6, MP7, MP8, CCSS.Math.Content.6.NS.B.2

CORE Ratio and Proportional Relationship Concepts

Understanding Ratios

UNPACK THE STANDARD
You will use ratios to describe the relationship between two quantities.

LEARN IT: A *ratio* is a comparison using two numbers. Ratios can compare a part to a part, a part to a whole, or a whole to a part. There are three ways to write a ratio: in word form, with a symbol (a colon), or as a fraction.

Example:

Part to Part:	**Part to Whole:**	**Whole to Part:**
The ratio of stars to triangles is six to three.	The ratio of triangles to the total number of shapes is 3 to 9.	The ratio of the total number of shapes to stars is nine to six.
think! There are 6 stars and 3 triangles.	**think!** There are 3 triangles and 9 shapes in all.	**think!** There are 9 shapes in all and 6 stars.
"six to three"	"three to nine"	"nine to six"
$6 : 3$	$3 : 9$	$9 : 6$
$\dfrac{6}{3}$	$\dfrac{3}{9}$	$\dfrac{9}{6}$

think! You can simplify ratios just as you would simplify a fraction! $\frac{6}{3}$ can be simplified to $\frac{2}{1}$, so this ratio in simplest form is 2:1. How would you simplify these other ratios?

PRACTICE: Now you try

Write each ratio three different ways.

Part to part.

1. There are 6 dogs to 4 cats.	2. There are 32 bikes to 16 scooters.

Part to whole.

3. There are 26 ice cream flavors in all, and 16 are chocolate flavored. **think!** Which is the part?	4. There are 40 students in the Math Club, and 17 are girls.

Whole to part.

5. There are 32 pets at the animal shelter, and 4 are birds. **think!** Which is the whole?	6. The science experiment uses 6 mL of liquid, 2 mL of which are vinegar.

Solve each ratio problem. Write your answer in any of the three forms. Are you comparing part to part, part to whole, or whole to part?

7. Mario uploaded 4 e-books and 6 games to his tablet. What is the ratio of e-books to games?	8. Aaron had eight friends over for his birthday party. Two of them were girls. What is the ratio of friends to girls?
9. There are 23 students and one teacher in Arianna's class. What is the ratio of students to teachers?	10. Josie uses 2 cups of milk and 3 cups of flour to make pancakes. What is the ratio of milk to flour in this recipe?

Raquel takes a poll in her class. Out of the 23 students, 14 like to play basketball, and the rest prefer volleyball. Write three ratios comparing these numbers: a part to a part, a part to a whole, and a whole to a part. Write each ratio in the three different ways. Show your work and write your explanation here.

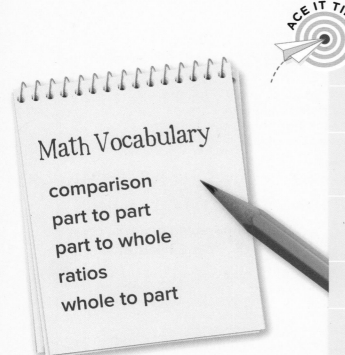

Math Vocabulary

comparison
part to part
part to whole
ratios
whole to part

	yes	no
Did you underline the question in the word problem?		
Did you circle the numbers or number words?		
Did you box the supporting details or information needed to solve the problem?		
Did you draw a picture or a graphic organizer and write a math sentence to show your thinking?		
Did you label your numbers and your picture?		
Did you explain your thinking and use math vocabulary words in your explanation?		

MATH ON THE MOVE

Make up your own ratios. Look for situations in real life where you can compare two numbers. Ratios are all around us!

Understanding Unit Rates

UNPACK THE STANDARD
You will compare and find equivalent ratios using tables and coordinate planes.

LEARN IT: A **rate** is a type of ratio in which the two numbers being compared are in different units. A **unit rate** is a ratio that compares a quantity to one.

Example: Rory paid $3 for 2 tacos. If each taco costs the same, how much did she pay for one taco?

Step 1:	Step 2:	Step 3:
Notice that the first term of the ratio is measured in dollars, and the second term is not. This means you are finding a rate, not just a ratio. **think!** Are all rates ratios? Are all ratios rates?	Write it as a ratio. $3 : 2 tacos or $\frac{3}{2}$	Divide. $\frac{3}{2} = 1.5$ It costs $1.50 per one taco.

We can also use a **tape diagram** to solve ratios.

Example: Andre baked 48 cookies in 4 minutes. How many cookies can he bake in 6 minutes?

```
|—— 48 cookies ——|
|   |   |   |   |
```
4 minutes

think! Draw 4 boxes to show 4 minutes. This shows the time to bake 48 cookies. 48 ÷ 4 = 12, so each box shows the time to bake 12 cookies.

Draw 6 boxes to show 6 minutes.

12 cookies	12 cookies	12 cookies	12 cookies	12 cookies	12 cookies

6 minutes

12 + 12 + 12 + 12 + 12 + 12 = 12 × 6 = 72 cookies

So, Andre can bake 72 cookies in 6 minutes.

PRACTICE: Now you try

Write a ratio for each problem. Find the unit rate.

1. $18 for 2 books that cost the same amount Ratio: _____ Unit Rate: _____	2. 28 miles in 7 minutes Ratio: _____ Unit Rate: _____
3. 16 lightning strikes in 4 minutes Ratio: _____ Unit Rate: _____	4. 92 students in 4 classes that have the same number of students per class Ratio: _____ Unit Rate: _____

Standard: CCSS.Math.Content.6.RP.A.1

5. Marc recorded 60 strikeouts in 12 baseball games. On average, how many strikeouts did he record per game?

6. Ashlee rode her bike 12 miles in 6 hours. If she rode the same number of miles each hour, how many miles per hour did she ride?

7. Mishka spent $40 on 8 books for her e-reader. Each book cost the same amount. What did she pay per book?

8. It takes Grant 24 minutes to run 8 laps. What is Grant's unit rate of laps per minute?

Julian's birthday party will cost $30 if he invites 6 friends. Assuming the same rate per friend invited, how many friends can he invite if he spends a total of $40 on his birthday party? *Hint:* Find the unit rate first. Show your work and explain your thinking on a piece of paper.

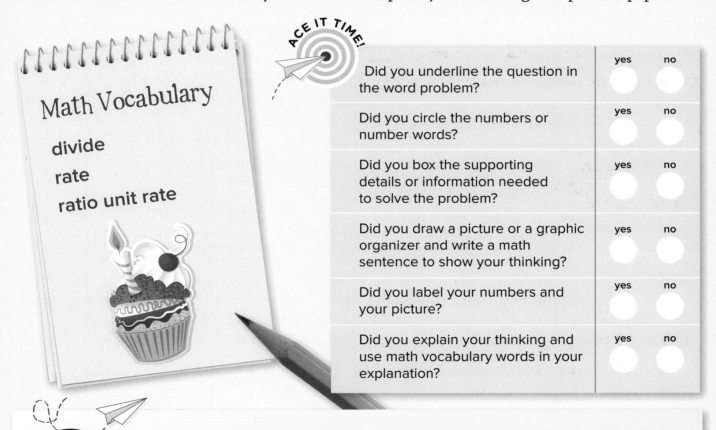

Math Vocabulary

divide

rate

ratio unit rate

ACE IT TIME!

	yes	no
Did you underline the question in the word problem?	○	○
Did you circle the numbers or number words?	○	○
Did you box the supporting details or information needed to solve the problem?	○	○
Did you draw a picture or a graphic organizer and write a math sentence to show your thinking?	○	○
Did you label your numbers and your picture?	○	○
Did you explain your thinking and use math vocabulary words in your explanation?	○	○

MATH ON THE MOVE

Think of ratios and rates you use in real-life situations. For example, how do you use unit rates at the gas station? How about with the gas mileage of a car? How many unit rates can you think of on your way to school?

Double Number Lines and Equivalent Ratios

UNPACK THE STANDARD
You will find equivalent ratios using a double number line.

LEARN IT: *Equivalent ratios* are ratios that have different numbers but the same number relationship. A *double number line* can be used to show equivalent ratios and solve problems.

Example: Mateo's healthy bread recipe calls for 5 cups of wheat flour for every 2 cups of soy flour. He uses a total of 20 cups of wheat flour to make bread. How many cups of soy flour does he use?

Step 1:

Draw two number lines one above the other. Label the number lines "Wheat flour" and "Soy flour."
Draw tick marks for 0. Then draw tick marks to show the given ratio.

wheat flour/soy flour = $\dfrac{5}{2}$

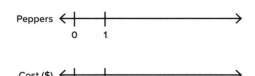

think! The quantities in each ratio are lined up, one above the other.

Step 2:

Use a pattern (+5) to extend the top number line to 20. Use a different pattern (+2) to extend the bottom line until it lines up with 20.

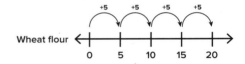

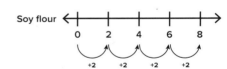

The ratio $\dfrac{20}{8}$ shows the answer.

Eight cups of soy flour are needed.

Example: Each pepper at a farm stand costs $0.40. How many peppers can be bought with $2.00?

Step 1:

Draw a double number line. Label the number lines "Peppers" and "Cost ($)". Draw tick marks for 0 and the given ratio, 1:0.40.

Step 2:

Use a pattern (+5) to extend the top number line to 20. Use a different pattern (+2) to extend the bottom line until it lines up with 20.

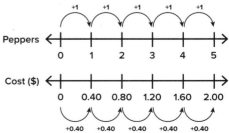

The ratio $\dfrac{5}{\$2.00}$ shows the answer.
Five peppers can be bought.

PRACTICE: Now you try

Label the double number lines. Use equivalent ratios to complete them. Then solve the problems.

1. Fruit punch has 4 liters of juice for every 3 liters of sparkling water. How many liters of sparkling water are needed if 24 liters of juice are used?

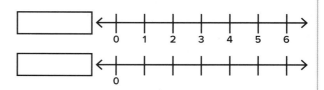

0   4   8   12   16   20   24

0

2. Each used book costs $0.50. How many used books can be bought with $1.50?

0   1   2   3   4   5   6

0

Omar charges $16 to mow 2 lawns. Make a double number line to show his earnings for mowing different numbers of lawns.
How many lawns must Omar mow to earn $96? Show your work and explain your thinking on a piece of paper.

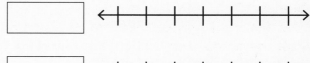
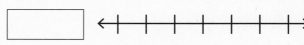

ACE IT TIME!

Math Vocabulary

double number line

equivalent ratio

rate

ratio

unit rate

	yes	no
Did you underline the question in the word problem?	◯	◯
Did you circle the numbers or number words?	◯	◯
Did you box the supporting details or information needed to solve the problem?	◯	◯
Did you draw a picture or a graphic organizer and write a math sentence to show your thinking?	◯	◯
Did you label your numbers and your picture?	◯	◯
Did you explain your thinking and use math vocabulary words in your explanation?	◯	◯

MATH ON THE MOVE

Find the unit price of items at a store. Make double number lines to show how the total cost changes depending on how many units or pounds are purchased. Experiment with the double number lines to see how changing the unit price affects total costs.

Tables and Equivalent Ratios

UNPACK THE STANDARD
You will compare and find equivalent ratios using tables and coordinate planes.

LEARN IT: Remember that equivalent ratios have different numbers but the same number relationship. Representing equivalent ratios in tables and on a coordinate plane can help you see patterns and understand how the ratios are related.

Example: Sarah is making loom bracelets. For every six red bands she uses, she uses three black bands. The table at right shows the relationship. Fill in the table to make equivalent ratios. Graph the ratios.

Red bands	2	4	6	8	10
Black bands			3		

Step 1:

What ratio does the problem give us?

$$\frac{\text{Red bands}}{\text{Black bands}} = \frac{6}{3}$$

Step 2:

Find the unit ratio.

$$\frac{6 \div ?}{3 \div ?} = \frac{?}{1}$$

$$\frac{6 \div 3}{3 \div 3} = \frac{2}{1}$$

The unit ratio is 2:1

Step 3:

Using the unit ratio, write equivalent ratios for the rest of the table.

$$\frac{2 \times 2 = 4}{1 \times 2 = 2}$$

$$\frac{2 \times 4 = 8}{1 \times 4 = 4}$$

$$\frac{2 \times 5 = 10}{1 \times 5 = 5}$$

think! Do the same to the numerator and denominator.

Step 4:

Complete the table.

Red bands	2	4	6	8	10
Black bands	1	2	3	4	5

Step 5:

List the ratios as ordered pairs.

(2, 1), (4, 2), (6, 3), (8, 4), (10, 5)

Step 6:

Plot the ordered pairs on a coordinate grid. Remember, *x* is the horizontal axis and *y* is the vertical axis. Plot your points in (*x*, *y*) order.

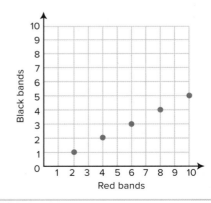

Standard: CCSS.Math.Content.6.RP.A. 3a

PRACTICE: Now you try

Use equivalent ratios to complete each table.

1.

Number of feet	35	70	105	140
Number of minutes	1			

2.

Number of pages	80	120	160	200
Number of books	2	3	4	5

3.

Number of apps	12	16	20	24
Number of folders			5	

4.

Number of people	16	32	48	64
Number of games				16

5.

Number of boys	3	6		12
Number of girls	7		21	

6.

Number of hours	4	8	12	16
Number of calls	13		39	52

It takes the Sandwich Shack 1 minute to prepare 4 sandwiches. Complete the table to find out how many minutes it takes to prepare 12, 16, and 20 sandwiches. After you complete the table, list the ordered pairs and plot on a coordinate grid on a separate sheet of paper.

Minutes	1	2			
Sandwiches	4	8			

ACE IT TIME!

	yes	no
Did you underline the question in the word problem?	○	○
Did you circle the numbers or number words?	○	○
Did you box the supporting details or information needed to solve the problem?	○	○
Did you draw a picture or a graphic organizer and write a math sentence to show your thinking?	○	○
Did you label your numbers and your picture?	○	○
Did you explain your thinking and use math vocabulary words in your explanation?	○	○

Math Vocabulary

coordinate grid
denominator
equivalent ratios
numerator
ordered pairs
table

MATH ON THE MOVE

Have a discussion with an adult or friend. What makes equivalent ratios similar to equivalent fractions? What makes them different? How does this information help you find equivalent ratios?

Understanding Unit Price and Constant Speed

UNPACK THE STANDARD
You will solve rate problems that use price and speed

LEARN IT: Imagine you are at the grocery store. You want to make smart choices about how you spend your money. You ask yourself, "Which items have better deals?" Use unit pricing to find the better deal. *Unit pricing* is how much something costs per unit. It helps us compare the overall cost.

Example: One 2-liter bottle of your favorite soda costs $1.40. If a 1-liter bottle of the same soda costs $0.99, which is the better deal?

Step 1:	Step 2:
Use division to find the cost per liter in the 2-liter bottle. This is the **unit rate.**	Compare.
$1.40 ÷ 2 liters = $0.70 per liter	The 2-liter bottle costs $0.70 per liter. The 1-liter bottle costs $0.99 per liter.
think! Use what you know about powers of ten to solve. If 14 ÷ 2 = 7, then 1.40 ÷ 2 = 0.70.	$0.70 < $0.99 The 2-liter bottle is a better deal!

You can use similar methods to calculate constant speed.

Example: It takes Landon 4 hours to ride his bike 24 miles. If he rides at a constant speed, what is the unit rate in miles per hour? How many miles will he have ridden in 6 hours?

Step 1:	Step 2:
Use division to find the unit rate.	Use the unit rate to solve.
24 miles ÷ 4 hours = 6 miles per hour	6 hours × 6 miles per hour = 36 miles
Landon rides at a constant speed of 6 miles per hour.	

PRACTICE: Now you try

Find each unit rate. Compare to find the better deal.

1. $3.25 for 5 songs or $1.80 for 2 songs	2. $2.00 for a pack of 5 tennis balls or $0.50 for two tennis balls

Standard: CCSS.Math.Content.6.RP.A. 3b

3. $6.50 for a 2-pound bag of trail mix or $8.00 for a 4-pound bag of trail mix	**4.** One six-pack of sports drink for $3.60 or 3 six-packs for $12.60

Find the constant speed to help you answer the questions.

5. Henry's family travels 350 miles in 5 hours, driving at a constant speed. How many miles per hour are they travelling?	**6.** Javier's puppy gained 12 pounds in 8 weeks. If he gained weight at a constant rate, how much weight did he gain each week?
7. Jamie walks 16 miles in 4 hours. At this rate, how many miles can she walk in 5 hours?	**8.** Shonda read 8 books in 4 months. At that rate, how many books will she have read in 6 months?

The Burger Hut sells 4 cheeseburgers for $5.00. Its competitor, Big Burgers, sells 6 cheeseburgers for $9.00. Which place offers the best price? Show your work and explain your thinking on a piece of paper.

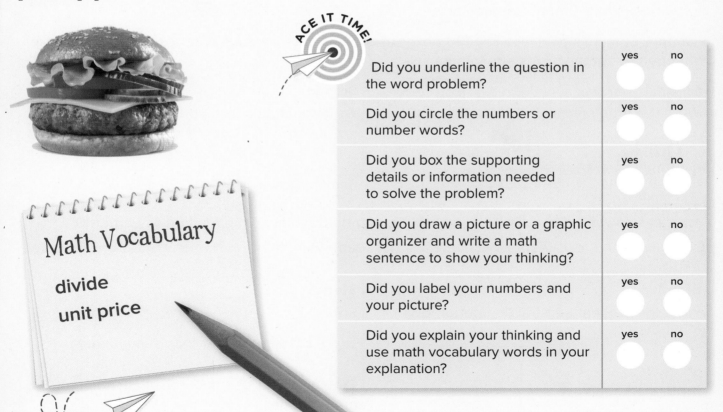

ACE IT TIME!

Math Vocabulary

divide

unit price

	yes	no
Did you underline the question in the word problem?	○	○
Did you circle the numbers or number words?	○	○
Did you box the supporting details or information needed to solve the problem?	○	○
Did you draw a picture or a graphic organizer and write a math sentence to show your thinking?	○	○
Did you label your numbers and your picture?	○	○
Did you explain your thinking and use math vocabulary words in your explanation?	○	○

MATH ON THE MOVE

The next time you go to a grocery store, do some math! Look at the price of each package of food to find the best deal. If you look closely, some stores will even list the unit price!

Identifying Percent

UNPACK THE STANDARD
You will write a percent as a fraction out of 100.

LEARN IT: A *percent* is a special ratio. It is a ratio per 100. 10% is ten parts out of 100. This is the same as $\frac{10}{100}$ or $\frac{1}{10}$ or 0.1.

If you get a 90% on a quiz, you are using this kind of rate.

WAIT! What if there aren't 100 questions on the quiz? This is what 90% on a quiz means: If you continued at your current rate until you finished 100 questions, you'd get 90 correct. And you'd be doing a great job!

Remember that fractions help you find *fractional parts* of whole numbers or groups. Since percentages can also be written as fractions, they can also find fractional parts. Use your knowledge from previous lessons and grades to write equivalent ratios and answer questions that use percentages.

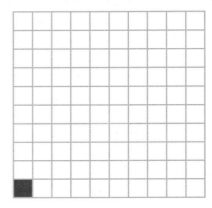

Example: Samara's goal is to sell 100 boxes of cookies in one year. So far, she has sold 65 boxes. What percent of the boxes did Samara sell?

Step 1:	**Step 2:**
Write the problem as a fraction out of 100.	Write the fraction as a percent.
think! Samara sold 65 out of 100 boxes of cookies. $\frac{65}{100}$	$\frac{65}{100}$ = 65% Samara has sold 65% of her cookies so far.

You can also write a percent as a fraction. Remember to think of the fraction as part of 100.

Example: Gino has 100 books at home. He has read 12% of them. How many of his books has he read?

Step 1:	**Step 2:**
Write the percent as a fraction out of 100. 12% = $\frac{12}{100}$	Solve. $\frac{12}{100}$ is 12 out of 100 (or the whole) Gino has read 12 books out of all the books he has at home.

PRACTICE: Now you try

Write the percent as a fraction.

1. 38%	2. 99%	3. 4%

Standard: CCSS.Math.Content.6.RP.A.3c

Write the fraction as a percent.

think!
Find the equivalent fraction to show per 100!

4. $\dfrac{16}{100}$	**5.** $\dfrac{7}{100}$	**6.** $\dfrac{80}{100}$

Solve the following problems.

7. In a survey of 100 students, 46 students said their favorite subject was science. What percent is that?	**8.** 35% of the first 100 customers at FroYo's put fresh fruit on their frozen yogurt. How many people is that?	**9.** In an art project, 6 out of 10 beads were turquoise. The rest were yellow. What percentage of the beads was turquoise? What percentage was yellow?

Horatio got 3 questions wrong on his spelling quiz. There were 10 questions on the quiz. He said he got 30% of the questions correct. Do you agree with him? Why or why not? Show your work and explain your thinking on a piece of paper.

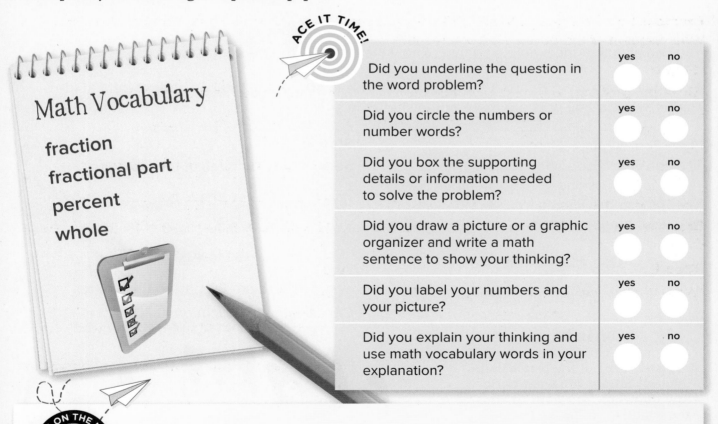

Math Vocabulary

fraction

fractional part

percent

whole

ACE IT TIME!

	yes	no
Did you underline the question in the word problem?	○	○
Did you circle the numbers or number words?	○	○
Did you box the supporting details or information needed to solve the problem?	○	○
Did you draw a picture or a graphic organizer and write a math sentence to show your thinking?	○	○
Did you label your numbers and your picture?	○	○
Did you explain your thinking and use math vocabulary words in your explanation?	○	○

MATH ON THE MOVE

Pay close attention to your grades at school! Look to see how your teacher uses percentages to grade your papers. How is it possible to get 90% on a test that only has 20 questions?

Finding Percent of a Number

UNPACK THE STANDARD
You will solve problems finding the percent of a given number.

LEARN IT: Sometimes you will be asked to find a percent of a number that is not 100. You can do this by using fractions.

Example: 60% of the songs on Jerry's tablet are Top 20 hits. If Jerry has 30 songs on his tablet, how many are Top 20 hits? Find 60% of 30.

Step 1:	**Step 2:**
Write an equivalent ratio to show the percentage as a fraction per 100.	Find the fractional part to solve. *Hint:* You multiply to find fractional parts.
60% is equal to 60 per 100	What is 60% of 30?
$$\frac{60}{100}$$	$$\frac{60}{100} \times \frac{30}{1} = \frac{1800}{100} = \frac{18}{1} = 18$$
	18 of Jerry's songs are Top 20 hits.

You can also find the whole when you know the *part* and the *percentage*.

Example: There are 32 cats at the pet shelter. This is 40% of the total number of pets at the shelter. How many pets are there at the shelter in all?

Step 1:	**Step 2:**
Decide which operation to use. What is the question asking you? *Remember, "of" means you are finding a fractional part, or multiplication!*	Solve. Use your rules of tens to help.
	40% = 0.40
32 is 40% of what number?	32 ÷ 0.40 = 320 ÷ 4 = 80
32 = 40% × _____	32 is 40% of 80.
	There are 80 pets in the shelter.
	Check with multiplication: 0.40 × 80 = 32

think!
32 is the part. Finding the fractional part of the whole uses multiplication. You want to do the opposite. You want to find the whole from the part. Which operation is the opposite of multiplication?

PRACTICE: Now you try

Find the percentages and numbers.

1. 50% of 900 = _____	2. 10% of 500 = _____	3. 20% of 30 = _____ *Hint:* What is 10% of 30? Use rules of tens to help!
4. 60% of 120 = _____	5. 90% of 200 = _____	6. 80% of 50 = _____
7. 36 is 60% of what number?	8. 18 is 20% of what number?	9. 56 is 70% of what number?

Cameron spent 70% of his birthday money at the mall. He spent $35 at the mall. How much money did he receive for his birthday? Show your work and explain your thinking on a piece of paper.

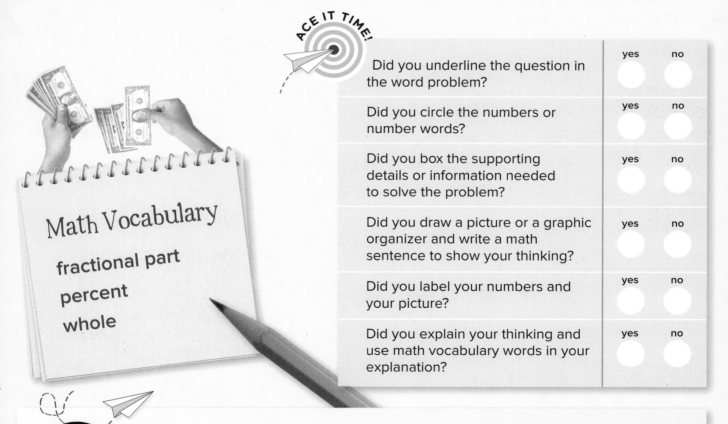

ACE IT TIME!

Math Vocabulary

fractional part

percent

whole

	yes	no
Did you underline the question in the word problem?	○	○
Did you circle the numbers or number words?	○	○
Did you box the supporting details or information needed to solve the problem?	○	○
Did you draw a picture or a graphic organizer and write a math sentence to show your thinking?	○	○
Did you label your numbers and your picture?	○	○
Did you explain your thinking and use math vocabulary words in your explanation?	○	○

MATH ON THE MOVE

What a sale! The next time you go shopping, look at the sales. Stores will often advertise things for a percentage off the original price, such as 20% off or 30% off. If a shirt costs $10, and the sale price is 20% off, how much would you save? *Hint:* If it is 20% off, you pay 80%.

Using Tape Diagrams with Percentages

UNPACK THE STANDARD
You will use tape diagrams to help you solve problems with percentages.

LEARN IT: Remember using tape diagrams with unit rates? A tape diagram divides a whole into equal parts, or percentages. We can also use tape diagrams to help us solve problems involving percentages and wholes.

Example: In a jar of 200 jellybeans, 30% of them are orange. How many of the jellybeans are orange? Find 30% of 200.

Step 1:
Write an expression for 30% of 200.

30% of 200 means 30% times 200.

30% of 200 = 30% × 200

Step 2:
Draw a tape diagram. Show 200 as the whole. Break it into 10 equal parts.

10%	20%	30%	40%	50%	60%	70%	80%	90%	100%

200 total jellybeans

Step 3:
Find the value of each part of the tape diagram.

10%	20%	30%	40%	50%	60%	70%	80%	90%	100%
20	40	60	80	100	120	140	160	180	200

200 total jellybeans

think!
200 divided into 10 equal parts gives us 20 in each box because 200 ÷ 10 = 20.

Step 4:
Solve. Shade all of the boxes up to 30% to find 30% of 200.

10%	20%	30%	40%	50%	60%	70%	80%	90%	100%
20	40	60	80	100	120	140	160	180	200

30% of 200 = 60, so there are 60 orange jellybeans in the jar.

think!
Does your answer make sense? Remember what the whole is!

PRACTICE: Now you try

Find the percentages and numbers.

1. 60% of 500 = _____

10%	20%	30%	40%	50%	60%	70%	80%	90%	100%
									500

2. 70% of 150 = _____

10%	20%	30%	40%	50%	60%	70%	80%	90%	100%
									150

Standard: CCSS.Math.Content.6.RP.A.3c

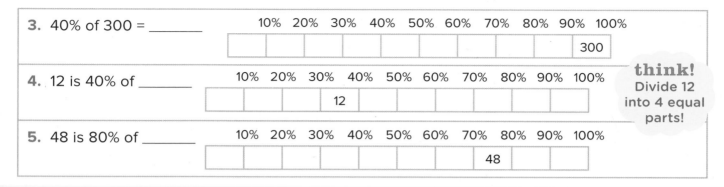

3. 40% of 300 = _____

	10%	20%	30%	40%	50%	60%	70%	80%	90%	100%
										300

4. 12 is 40% of _____

	10%	20%	30%	40%	50%	60%	70%	80%	90%	100%
				12						

think!
Divide 12 into 4 equal parts!

5. 48 is 80% of _____

	10%	20%	30%	40%	50%	60%	70%	80%	90%	100%
								48		

There are 22 students in Mrs. Hale's sixth-grade algebra class. That is 20% of all the sixth graders in the whole school. How many sixth-grade students are there in the whole school? Use the tape diagram below to help you solve. Show your work and explain your thinking on a piece of paper.

	10%	20%	30%	40%	50%	60%	70%	80%	90%	100%
	22									

ACE IT TIME!

	yes	no
Did you underline the question in the word problem?	○	○
Did you circle the numbers or number words?	○	○
Did you box the supporting details or information needed to solve the problem?	○	○
Did you draw a picture or a graphic organizer and write a math sentence to show your thinking?	○	○
Did you label your numbers and your picture?	○	○
Did you explain your thinking and use math vocabulary words in your explanation?	○	○

Math Vocabulary

part
percentages
tape diagram
whole

MATH ON THE MOVE

Talk about it! Explain to a friend or an adult how using tape diagrams can be helpful when working with percentages.

Ratios and Unit Conversions

UNPACK THE STANDARD
You will use ratios to convert measurements.

LEARN IT: You can use ratios to compare measurements in both the Customary and Metric System. Use what you know about each unit of measurement, or use a conversion chart to help you.

Example: Which is longer: 5 feet or 65 inches?

Step 1:	Step 2:	Step 3:
Decide which unit to convert. Let's go from feet to inches. Write the ratio for feet to inches. 1 foot = 12 inches $\frac{feet}{inches} = \frac{1}{12}$	Write an equivalent ratio to show the number of inches in 5 feet. $\frac{feet}{inches} = \frac{1}{12} = \frac{5}{?}$	Solve. $\frac{1 \times 5}{12 \times 5} = \frac{5}{60}$ 5 feet = 60 inches 65 inches > 60 inches 65 inches is longer than 5 feet.

You can also use a table to help you find the equivalent ratios.
Example: Which has a greater capacity: 3 liters or 2,000 milliliters?

Step 1:	Step 2:
Create a table. Look for patterns in the equivalent ratios. The ratio of liters to milliliters is 1:1,000. 	L	1	2	3	4
mL	1,000	2,000	3,000	4,000		Decide which units to compare. Let's compare mL. 3 L = 3,000 mL 3,000 mL > 2,000 mL 3 L is a higher capacity than 2,000 mL.

PRACTICE: Now you try

Use ratios to convert each measurement. Use a conversion chart to help you solve.

1. 3 yd = _____ ft	**2.** 4 days = _____ hrs	**3.** 16 qts = _____ gal
4. 70 mm = _____ cm	**5.** 8 kg = _____ g	**6.** 6 km = _____ m

Standard: CCSS.Math.Content.6.RP.A.3d

Compare. Write >, <, or =.

7. 4 yd ◯ 152 in.	**8.** 3 lb ◯ 48 oz	**9.** 5 min ◯ 260 s
10. 6,000 mm ◯ 60 cm	**11.** 400 mg ◯ 3 g	**12.** 25 L ◯ 2 kL
13. The laptops at Kenzy's school weigh 3,000 grams each. The laptop she uses at home weighs 2.75 kilograms. Which laptop is lighter?	**14.** Which podcast lasts longer: one that is 2 hours and 15 minutes long or one that is 125 minutes long?	**15.** The track at Cortez Middle School is 200 meters long. How many times would you need to walk the track to walk 1 kilometer? *Hint:* How many meters in 1 kilometer?

Micheala has 1,900 mm of twine for making friendship bracelets. She wants to make 2 bracelets to share with her friend. Each bracelet needs 92 cm of twine. What ratio should she use to find out if she has enough twine for both bracelets? Does she have enough? How do you know? Show your work and explain your thinking on a piece of paper.

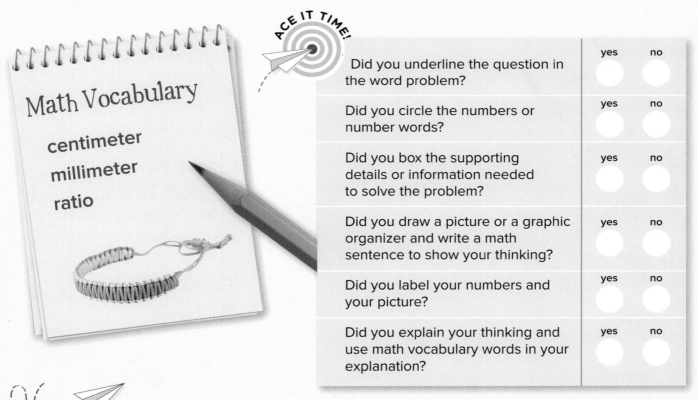

ACE IT TIME!

Math Vocabulary

centimeter

millimeter

ratio

	yes	no
Did you underline the question in the word problem?	◯	◯
Did you circle the numbers or number words?	◯	◯
Did you box the supporting details or information needed to solve the problem?	◯	◯
Did you draw a picture or a graphic organizer and write a math sentence to show your thinking?	◯	◯
Did you label your numbers and your picture?	◯	◯
Did you explain your thinking and use math vocabulary words in your explanation?	◯	◯

MATH ON THE MOVE Measurement conversions are everywhere! Each time you see a measurement unit, ask yourself how you can use a ratio to convert it to a different measurement. Be sure to stay within either the Customary or the Metric System.

Stop and think about what you have learned.

Congratulations! You've finished the lessons for this unit. This means you've learned about ratios and how they can be used to compare two quantities. You've learned that a rate is a special kind of ratio, and also how to find a unit rate, especially when solving problems that use price and speed. You've seen the relationship between equivalent fractions and ratios and percent. You've even learned how to use ratios to convert units of measurement.

Now it's time to prove your skills with ratios. Solve the problems below! Use all of the methods you have learned.

Activity Section 1: Understanding Ratios

Fill in the blanks and answer the questions.

1. A bowl of fruit has 4 apples, 3 bananas, and 2 oranges. Write the following ratios:

   a. Bananas to apples:

   b. Apples to bananas:

   c. Bananas to oranges:

   d. Oranges to apples:

2. The parking lot at your school has 12 scooters, 22 cars, and 38 SUVs. Write the following ratios:

   a. Scooters to cars:

   b. Cars to SUVs:

   c. Scooters to total vehicles:

   d. Total vehicles to SUVs:

3. Out of the 32 apps on Jaylen's tablet, 12 are science related. What is the ratio of science-related apps to the total number of apps on Jaylen's tablet?

4. Of the 22 students in Mr. Maguire's class, 4 are left-handed. What is the ratio of left-handed students to right-handed students?

5. Colton's baseball team has 14 members. 5 players have to sit the bench each inning. What is the ratio of the number of team members playing to those sitting the bench each inning?

Standards: CCSS.Math.Content.6.RP.A.1, 6.RP.A.2, 6.RP.A.3a, 6.RP.A. 3b, 6.RP.A.3c, 6.RP.A.3d

Activity Section 2: Understanding Unit Rates

Solve the following problems.

1. Gregg spent $45.00 on 2 t-shirts. Each t-shirt was the same price. What is the unit rate of each t-shirt?	**2.** Amir paid $4.50 for 2 pounds of grapes. What is the unit rate for 1 pound of grapes?
3. A city bus traveled 54 miles in 3 hours, including stops. What is the unit rate per hour?	**4.** Three full airplanes hold 570 people. How many people can 1 airplane hold?
5. A cake recipe calls for 4 eggs to 2 cups of milk. What is the number of eggs per cup of milk for this recipe? 	

Activity Section 3: Double Number Lines and Equivalent Ratios

Solve the following problems using double number lines.

1. Each song download cost $1.25. How many songs can you download for $5.00?

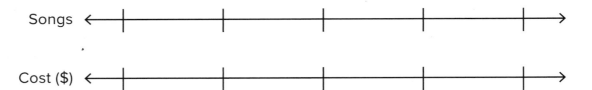

Songs

Cost ($)

2. For every 4 hours of babysitting, Coreen makes $32.00. How much money will she earn if she babysits for 6 hours?

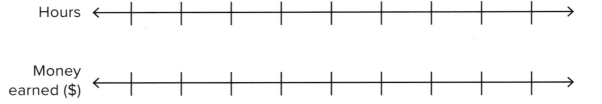

Hours

Money earned ($)

Standards: CCSS.Math.Content.6.RP.A.1, 6.RP.A.2, 6.RP.A.3a, 6.RP.A. 3b, 6.RP.A.3c, 6.RP.A.3d

Activity Section 4: Tables and Equivalent Ratios

Fill in the blanks of each table.

1.

Number of hours	3	9	15	24
Number of miles	8			

2.

Number of CDs	1	2	3	4
Number of songs			36	

3.

Number of boys	Number of girls
4	
8	
24	48
32	

4.

Number of jeeps	Number of riders
2	
4	
6	
8	32

5a.

Number of months	Number of books read
1	
2	
3	6
4	
5	

5c. Plot the ordered pairs on the coordinate plane.

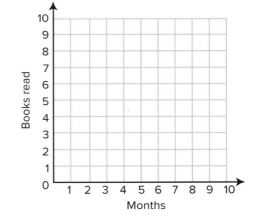

5b. List the ratios in the table as ordered pairs.

_____

_____

_____

_____

_____

6. Which of the following ratios is NOT equivalent to the ratio $\frac{3}{4}$?

A. $\frac{6}{8}$ B. $\frac{15}{20}$ Explain: _____

C. $\frac{30}{40}$ D. $\frac{3}{8}$ _____

Activity Section 5: Understanding Unit Price and Constant Speed

Solve the following problems.

1. It costs $6.25 for 5 packs of gum. If each pack costs the same, what is the unit price for one pack of gum?
2. Josh bought 4 smartphone cases for $28. What is the unit price of each case? At that price, how much will 5 cases cost?
3. For Carrie's art project, she uses 2 tubes of white paint for every 4 tubes of blue paint. At that rate, how many tubes of white paint will she use if she uses 12 tubes of blue paint?
4. It takes Jeremiah 2 minutes to run 4 laps around the track. At that rate, how long will it take for him to run 8 laps around the track?
5. Keenan rode her bicycle 12 miles in 2 hours. She rides at a constant speed. What is her unit rate in miles per hour? How many miles will she have ridden in 4 hours?

Activity Section 6: Identifying Percent

Fill in the blanks and answer the questions.

1. 65 out of 100 = _____ %	2. 13 out of 100 = _____ %
3. $\frac{42}{100}$ = _____ %	4. $\frac{5}{100}$ = _____ %
5. $\frac{6}{10}$ = _____ %	6. $\frac{2}{10}$ = _____ %

Write the percent as a fraction.

7. 11%	8. 91%
9. 3%	10. 66%

Standards: CCSS.Math.Content.6.RP.A.1, 6.RP.A.2, 6.RP.A.3a, 6.RP.A. 3b, 6.RP.A.3c, 6.RP.A.3d

Activity Section 7: Finding Percent of a Number

Solve the following problems.

1. 20% of 60 = _____	2. 70% of 20 = _____	3. 80% of 300 = _____
4. 15 is 10% of what number?	5. 20 is 20% of what number?	6. 120 is 40% of what number?
7. In a package of trail mix, 20% of the mix is walnuts. If 16 of the pieces in the trail mix are walnuts, how many pieces are in the trail mix?	8. 60% of the movies showing in the movie theater are comedies. If the theater is playing 15 movies, how many of them are comedies?	

Activity Section 8: Using Tape Diagrams with Percentages

Solve the following problems using the tape diagrams.

1. 40% of 400 = _____

10%	20%	30%	40%	50%	60%	70%	80%	90%	100%

2. 60% of 150 = _____

10%	20%	30%	40%	50%	60%	70%	80%	90%	100%

3. 18 is 60% of _____

10%	20%	30%	40%	50%	60%	70%	80%	90%	100%
					18				

Activity Section 9: Ratios and Unit Conversions

Fill in the blanks and answer the questions. Use a conversion chart.

1. 6,000 mg = _____ g	2. 55 km = _____ m	3. 45 ft = _____ yd
4. 4,000 mL = _____ L	5. 5 gal = _____ qt	6. 80 oz = _____ lb
7. 2 tons = _____ lb	8. 12 ft = _____ in.	9. 4 ft 7 in. = _____ in.
10. 300 mm = _____ cm	11. 200 cm = _____ m	12. 3 mi = _____ ft

Compare. Write >, <, or =.

13. 2 km ◯ 250 m	14. 3 lb ◯ 41 oz	15. 350 mg ◯ 3 g
16. 450 L ◯ 4 kL	17. 8 qt ◯ 2 gal	18. 800 mm ◯ 8 cm
19. 14 ft ◯ 3 yd	20. 60 in. ◯ 5 ft	21. 3 kg ◯ 300 g
22. 400 cm ◯ 4 m	23. 16 pt. ◯ 3 c	24. 3,000 lb ◯ 2 tons

Standards: CCSS.Math.Content.6.RP.A.1, 6.RP.A.2, 6.RP.A.3a, 6.RP.A. 3b, 6.RP.A.3c, 6.RP.A.3d

UNDERSTAND

Understand the meaning of what you have learned and apply your knowledge.

Sometimes you are given a percentage and a part of a whole and asked to find the whole. You will need to have an understanding of number sense, fractions, and powers of 10 to solve ratio problems like these.

Activity Section

Shakir's family is driving to their family reunion. They have traveled 80 miles so far, and 40% of their trip is complete. How many total miles is their trip? Explain your work in the space below.

DISCOVER

You use ratios whenever you compare numbers. Real-world situations can help you understand ratios better.

Activity Section

1. Fill in the table below using the information in the nutrition label and answer the questions.

Number of servings	1	2	3	4
Sugars (in grams)	8			

HONEY-O CEREAL

Nutrition Facts

Serving size: 1 cup

Amount Per Serving	
Calories: 110	
Total Fat	1g
Total Carbohydrates	22 g
Dietary Fiber	6 g
Sugars	8 g
Protein	2 g
Potassium	200 mg

a. What is the unit rate of sugar per serving of Honey-O Cereal? _____

b. How many grams of sugar are in 5 servings of Honey-O Cereal? _____

2. What is the ratio of carbohydrates to protein in one serving of Honey-O Cereal? How many grams of carbohydrates are in 2 servings? 4 servings?

3. Fill in the table below:

Serving Size (in cups)	1	2	3	4
Protein (in grams)	2			

4. What is the unit rate of protein per cup of Honey-O Cereal? _____

5. One serving of Honey-O Cereal is 20% of your daily recommended serving of dietary fiber.

a. How many total grams of dietary fiber is the daily recommendation? _____

b. How many servings of Honey-O Cereal would you need to eat each day to reach the daily recommended serving of dietary fiber? _____

Dividing Fractions

UNPACK THE STANDARD
You will divide fractions by other fractions.

LEARN IT: You know how to divide a fraction by a whole number and vice versa. Now you're going to divide fractions by other fractions.

One way to divide fractions is with a visual model, like a number line.

Example: Elisa saws a piece of wood that is $\frac{2}{3}$ yard long into pieces. Each piece is $\frac{1}{6}$ yard. How many pieces will she have?

Step 1:	**Step 2:**
Draw a number line showing 0 to 1 yard. Shade it to represent the total length of the piece of wood ($\frac{2}{3}$ yard). 	Divide the number line into sixths to represent the size of each piece. 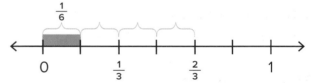

Step 3:

Count. How many $\frac{1}{6}$ pieces fit into $\frac{2}{3}$? There are four $\frac{1}{6}$ pieces in $\frac{2}{3}$.

Elisa will have four $\frac{1}{6}$-yard pieces of wood.

You can also divide fractions by multiplying. Remember that multiplying and dividing are opposites. **Reciprocals** are numbers that can be multiplied to get a product of 1. Dividing by a number is the same as multiplying by the reciprocal.

How do you find a reciprocal? Reciprocals are found by flipping (or inverting) the numerator and denominator. For example, 6 and $\frac{1}{6}$ are reciprocals because $\frac{6}{1} \times \frac{1}{6} = \frac{6}{6} = 1$.

Example: $\frac{2}{3} \div \frac{1}{6} = 4$

Step 1:	Step 2:
Find the reciprocal of the divisor.	Multiply the dividend by the reciprocal.
think! The divisor is $\frac{1}{6}$. The reciprocal is $\frac{6}{1}$.	$\frac{2}{3} \times \frac{6}{1} = \frac{12}{3} = 4$
Remember, dividend ÷ divisor = quotient.	*Remember, multiply the numerators together and the denominators together*

PRACTICE: Now you try

Divide to find the quotient. Don't forget to simplify!

1. $\frac{3}{6} \div \frac{1}{6}$	2. $\frac{2}{3} \div \frac{5}{6}$	3. $\frac{3}{5} \div \frac{2}{4}$
4. $\frac{1}{3} \div \frac{1}{2}$	5. $\frac{6}{8} \div 3$	6. $\frac{4}{12} \div \frac{2}{6}$

7. How many $\frac{1}{8}$-pound turkey burgers can be made from $\frac{3}{4}$ pound of ground turkey?	8. Rob has $\frac{3}{4}$ quart of orange juice. He pours $\frac{2}{8}$ quart into each glass at breakfast. How many glasses of orange juice can he serve?

Leeza has a piece of ribbon she wants to use for her Spirit Day costume at school. The ribbon is $\frac{5}{8}$ meter long. She wants to cut it into pieces that are $\frac{1}{8}$ meter long. How many pieces will she have? Show your work and write your explanation here.

Math Vocabulary

divisor
dividend
reciprocal

ACE IT TIME!

	yes	no
Did you underline the question in the word problem?	○	○
Did you circle the numbers or number words?	○	○
Did you box the supporting details or information needed to solve the problem?	○	○
Did you draw a picture or a graphic organizer and write a math sentence to show your thinking?	○	○
Did you label your numbers and your picture?	○	○
Did you explain your thinking and use math vocabulary words in your explanation?	○	○

Roll dice to make up your own fraction division problems! Roll one die 4 times to get 4 numbers. Decide where to place each number (either the numerator or denominator) to create 2 fractions. Divide the fractions by changing the divisor to its reciprocal!

Dividing with Mixed Numbers

UNPACK THE STANDARD
You will divide with mixed numbers.

LEARN IT: Do you remember how to multiply mixed numbers? First, you convert each mixed number into an improper fraction (a fraction greater than one). Then you multiply. Use this same process to divide with mixed numbers.

Example: A crate weighing $13\frac{1}{3}$ pounds contains packages of skateboard wheels that weigh $3\frac{1}{3}$ pounds each. How many packages are in the crate?

Step 1:	Step 2:	Step 3:
Rewrite each mixed number as an improper fraction. $$13\frac{1}{3} = \frac{40}{3}$$ $$3\frac{1}{3} = \frac{10}{3}$$ **think!** Multiply the denominator by the whole number and add the numerator.	Set up the division problem. $$\frac{40}{3} \div \frac{10}{3}$$ 	Use reciprocals and solve. $$\frac{40}{3} \div \frac{10}{3} = \frac{40}{3} \times \frac{3}{10}$$ $$= \frac{120}{30}$$ $$= 4$$ There are 4 packages in the crate.

You can use a short cut when multiplying fractions. Let's use the problem above: $\frac{40}{3} \times \frac{3}{10}$

You can simplify by common factors. Notice how the numerator of each fraction is diagonally "connected" to the denominator of the other fraction by the lines in the multiplication sign. You can simplify these factors before multiplying if they share a similar factor.

$$\frac{40}{3} \times \frac{3}{10} = \frac{4}{1} \times \frac{1}{1} = 4$$

think! What number do you divide 40 and 10 by to get 4 and 1? Why does this work? *Hint:* You simplified the product 120/30 above by dividing numerator and denominator by the same number.

PRACTICE: Now you try

Find each quotient.

1. $3\frac{1}{2} \div 2\frac{1}{2}$	2. $3\frac{3}{4} \div 1\frac{1}{8}$	3. $4 \div 1\frac{1}{3}$	**think!** Rewrite 4 as a fraction to help you solve!
4. $3\frac{3}{9} \div 2\frac{2}{6}$	5. $4\frac{1}{2} \div 2\frac{1}{4}$	6. $3\frac{3}{7} \div 2\frac{2}{3}$	

7. You and three friends share $4\frac{1}{2}$ liters of sports drink equally. How much drink will each of you receive?

8. Maxwell has a wooden board that is $7\frac{1}{2}$ yards long. He wants to cut it into pieces that are $2\frac{1}{2}$ yards each. How many pieces will he end up with?

Mr. Elton has $4\frac{4}{5}$ pounds of clay for the students in his pottery class. He will divide the clay into $\frac{1}{5}$-pound portions. How many portions of clay will he have? Will he have enough for the 22 students in his pottery class? Show your work and write your explanation here.

ACE IT TIME!

	yes	no
Did you underline the question in the word problem?	○	○
Did you circle the numbers or number words?	○	○
Did you box the supporting details or information needed to solve the problem?	○	○
Did you draw a picture or a graphic organizer and write a math sentence to show your thinking?	○	○
Did you label your numbers and your picture?	○	○
Did you explain your thinking and use math vocabulary words in your explanation?	○	○

Math Vocabulary

divide
improper fractions
mixed numbers
multiply
reciprocal

MATH ON THE MOVE

Talk with an adult or friend about dividing mixed numbers. How can you use what you know about multiplying fractions? Why does simplifying before multiplying make your work simpler?

REVIEW

Stop and think about what you have learned.

Congratulations! You've finished the lessons for this unit. This means you've learned about dividing fractions! You can divide fractions using number lines and reciprocals. You've also learned how to divide mixed numbers.

Now it's time to prove your skills with fractions. Solve the problems below! Use all of the methods you have learned.

Activity Section 1: Dividing Fractions

Solve the following problems.

1. $\frac{3}{4} \div \frac{3}{12}$	2. $\frac{3}{5} \div \frac{4}{5}$	3. $\frac{3}{3} \div \frac{6}{9}$
4. $\frac{4}{5} \div \frac{2}{10}$	5. $\frac{9}{10} \div \frac{4}{5}$	6. $\frac{3}{15} \div \frac{3}{5}$

7. How many $\frac{1}{4}$-pound bags can be poured from a $\frac{9}{12}$-pound bag of trail mix?

8. Gia has a $\frac{1}{2}$ quart of milk. She fills 4 glasses. How much milk will she pour into each glass?

9. Some friends run in a relay race that is $\frac{3}{4}$ of a mile long. Each runner runs $\frac{1}{8}$ of a mile. How many runners are in the relay race?

Standard: CCSS.Math.Content.6.NS.A.1

10. What is the reciprocal of the number 2? _____ How do you know? _____

_____

_____

11. Explain the steps you would take to solve the problem $\frac{3}{4} \div \frac{1}{3}$ _____

_____

_____

_____

_____

12. Which problem can be solved using the expression $2\frac{2}{3} \div \frac{3}{4}$?

   A. Angie ate $\frac{2}{3}$ of a container that holds $\frac{3}{4}$ of a cup of frozen yogurt.
       How much frozen yogurt did she eat?

   B. Angie ate $\frac{3}{4}$ of a container that holds $2\frac{2}{3}$ cups of frozen yogurt.
       How much frozen yogurt did she eat?

   C. How many $\frac{3}{4}$-cup servings are in $2\frac{2}{3}$ cups of frozen yogurt?

   D. How many $\frac{2}{3}$-cup servings are in $\frac{3}{4}$ of a cup of frozen yogurt?

Explain how you know: _____

_____

_____

_____

_____

Activity Section 2: Dividing with Mixed Numbers

Solve the following problems.

1. $3\frac{1}{2} \div \frac{1}{4}$	2. $4\frac{2}{3} \div 2$	3. $6\frac{6}{8} \div 2\frac{1}{4}$
4. $4\frac{2}{5} \div 2\frac{1}{5}$	5. $12\frac{1}{2} \div \frac{5}{6}$	6. $7 \div 1\frac{2}{8}$

7. Rhianna has a board that is $1\frac{4}{8}$ meters long. She wants to cut it into three equal pieces. How long will each piece be?

8. How many equal-sized pieces can you cut from a $9\frac{1}{3}$-foot piece of rope if each piece is $1\frac{1}{6}$ feet long?

9. Kylie is filling the bird feeder in her backyard. It holds a total of $2\frac{1}{2}$ cups of bird seed. The scoop she is using holds $\frac{1}{4}$ cup of bird seed. How many scoops will she use to fill the bird feeder?

10. A rectangular plot of land has an area of $1\frac{1}{2}$ square kilometers and a length of $\frac{3}{4}$ kilometer. What is the width of this plot of land? *Hint:* Think about the formula $A = l \times w$. How do you find w if you know A and l? Draw a picture and explain your thinking.

UNDERSTAND

When you divide, you are performing the opposite of multiplication. Think about what you know about opposites in mathematics. Find the opposite of the opposite of 3: -(-3). This equals 3!

When you divide fractions, you multiply by the reciprocal of the divisor. This is using the opposite of an opposite! That's why the answer is correct, even though you are changing the operation you use.

Activity Section

Joel found a board in his backyard that was $\frac{5}{6}$ of a yard long. He wanted to use it to help fix his treehouse. $\frac{1}{3}$ of a yard of the board was damaged, so he cut that part off. Then he cut what remained into pieces that were each $\frac{1}{6}$ of a yard long. How many pieces did he have to fix his treehouse? Explain how you got your answer.

Discover how you can apply the information you have learned.

You use mixed numbers every day. Dividing mixed numbers uses the same process as dividing fractions. Use what you know about operations with fractions to solve. Don't forget to simplify!

Activity Section

Dione hikes a trail that is $3\frac{3}{4}$ miles long. She stops to rest every $1\frac{1}{4}$ mile. Jeremy hikes the same trail and stops to rest twice. He says he stopped for fewer breaks than Dione did. Is he correct? How do you know?

Standards: CCSS.Math.Content.6.NS.A.1, CCSS.Math.Practice.MP1, MP2, MP3, MP4, MP6, MP7, MP8

CORE Number System Operation Concepts

Division Review

UNPACK THE STANDARD
You will divide multi-digit whole numbers using the standard algorithm.

LEARN IT: Let's review the standard algorithm. Think about what you already know: The standard algorithm uses place value to simplify division. It is a quick way of doing partial products.

Example: The shuttle at Los Angeles International Airport takes 7,132 people from the main terminal to terminal B. The shuttle can hold 35 people. How many trips does it need to take?

Step 1: Find the thousands place of the quotient.

Since 35 does not go into 7, there are 0 thousands in the quotient.

Step 2: Find the hundreds place of the quotient.

Remember your patterns of tens. To find 7,100 ÷ 35, you can treat this as 71 ÷ 35.

71 ÷ 35 = 2 plus some left over

7,100 ÷ 35 = 200 plus some left over

```
                2  0  3  r 27
       35 ) 7   1  3  2
          -  7  0
                1  3
              -    0
                1  3  2
              - 1  0  5
                   2  7
```

Step 3: Repeat with the tens and ones. 7,132 ÷ 35 = 203 remainder 27

Step 4: Interpret the remainder. Think about what the question is asking you. If the shuttle only takes 203 trips, 27 people will be left in the main terminal. Round up to 204 to find the total number of trips the shuttle takes to move all of the people.

Remember to check your answer by multiplying!

```
      203
  ×    35
    1,015
  + 6,090
    7,105
  +    27
    7,132
```

PRACTICE: Now you try

Divide to find the quotient.

1. $29\overline{)929}$	**2.** $43\overline{)4,427}$
3. $4,789 \div 15$	**4.** $2,884 \div 24$
5. A factory packages 1,620 cellphones in 60 minutes. How many cellphones can it package in one minute? **think!** Is this the same as finding a unit rate?	**6.** The Good Eats Restaurant unpacks 2,562 napkins into napkin holders. Each napkin holder can hold 125 napkins. How many napkin holders do they need?

A snack food company produced 5,929 ounces of dried fruit snacks. The company will put the fruit snacks into 16-ounce packages. How many packages will the company be able to fill? Be sure to interpret the remainder, if there is one. Check your answer with multiplication! Show your work and write your explanation here.

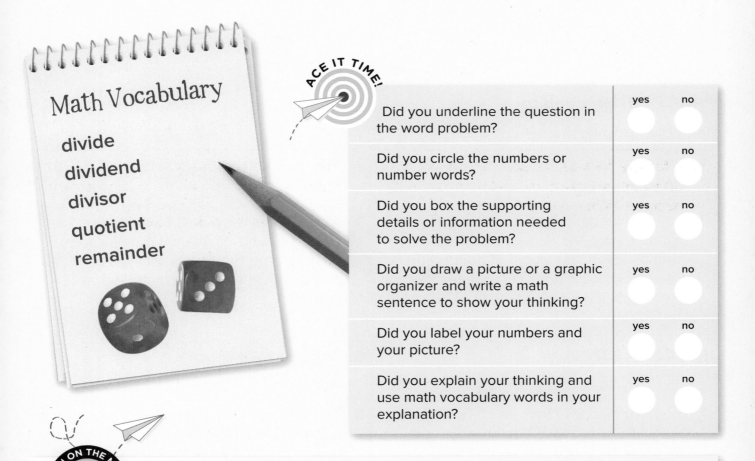

Math Vocabulary

divide
dividend
divisor
quotient
remainder

ACE IT TIME!

	yes	no
Did you underline the question in the word problem?		
Did you circle the numbers or number words?		
Did you box the supporting details or information needed to solve the problem?		
Did you draw a picture or a graphic organizer and write a math sentence to show your thinking?		
Did you label your numbers and your picture?		
Did you explain your thinking and use math vocabulary words in your explanation?		

MATH ON THE MOVE

Roll the dice! Roll a die 6 times to create a 4-digit dividend and a 2-digit divisor. Solve!

Adding Decimals

UNPACK THE STANDARD
You will add multi-digit decimals using the standard algorithm.

LEARN IT: Do you remember the most important part about adding decimals? Right! Line up the decimal points!

Example: So far this month, Jameel has run 3.255 miles. Last month, he ran 23.54 miles. How many miles has he run all together in these two months so far?

Step 1:	Step 2:
Write the problem vertically, and line up the decimal points.	Add as you normally would with whole numbers. Start in the place all the way to the right (in this case, the thousandths place).

Step 1:

$$\begin{array}{r} 3.255 \\ + \ 23.540 \\ \hline \end{array}$$

think! You can put a 0 here without changing the value of the number. .54 is equivlent to .540.

Step 2:

$$\begin{array}{r} 3.255 \\ + \ 23.540 \\ \hline 26.795 \end{array}$$

PRACTICE: Now you try

Solve the following problems.

1. 201.4 + 0.447	2. 7.89 + 135.85
3. Nate rescued a dog that weighed 16.8 pounds. Lucy, the dog, gained 2.25 pounds in the first month at home with Nate. How much does Lucy weigh after her first month at home?	4. Jordan rides the bus 13.85 miles to school every morning. He lives 0.75 miles from the bus stop. How many total miles does Jordan travel each morning to get to school?
5. 64.251 + 232.00	6. 782.6 + 82.178
7. Brooklyn paid $6.75 for lunch on Saturday. Then, she spent $0.99 on an ice cream bar. How much did she spend in all?	8. The O'Hare family drove 469.5 miles from Atlanta, GA to New Orleans, LA. Then they drove 508.32 miles from New Orleans to Austin, TX. How many miles did they travel in all?

Standard: CCSS.Math.Content.6.NS.B.3

Ricardo recorded the height of a plant for his science experiment. In week 1, the plant was 4.576 cm tall. In week 2, the plant had grown 1.7 cm. In week 3, the plant grew 2.45 cm. How tall was the plant after the third week? Show your work and write your explanation here.

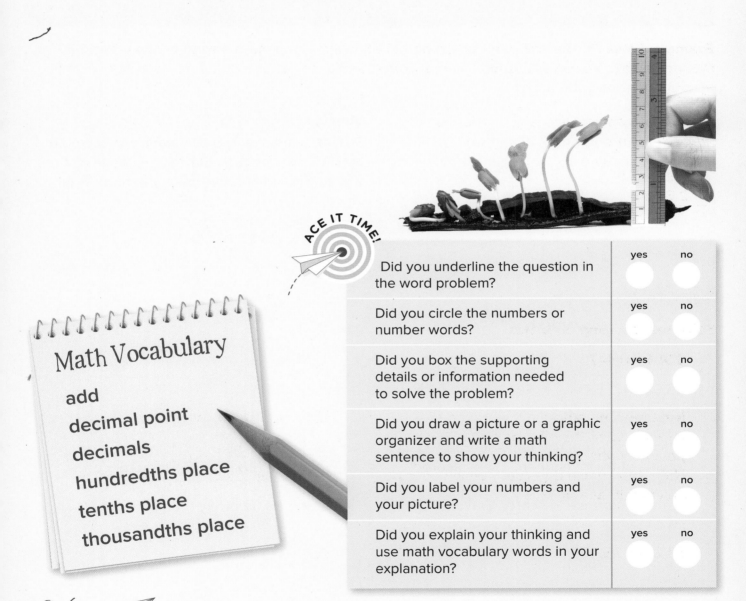

Math Vocabulary

add
decimal point
decimals
hundredths place
tenths place
thousandths place

ACE IT TIME!

	yes	no
Did you underline the question in the word problem?	○	○
Did you circle the numbers or number words?	○	○
Did you box the supporting details or information needed to solve the problem?	○	○
Did you draw a picture or a graphic organizer and write a math sentence to show your thinking?	○	○
Did you label your numbers and your picture?	○	○
Did you explain your thinking and use math vocabulary words in your explanation?	○	○

MATH ON THE MOVE

Roll the dice! Roll a die three times. Create a decimal with those three numbers. Place the decimal point wherever you like! Roll the die three more times to create another decimal. This time, place the decimal in a different place. Find the sum!

Subtracting Decimals

UNPACK THE STANDARD
You will subtract multi-digit decimals using the standard algorithm.

LEARN IT: Let's review how to subtract decimals. Remember, it is just like subtracting whole numbers, but you line the decimal points up.

Example: Wow! After a few years of saving her allowance, Terezka's saving account had $207.90. She decided to spend $42.79 on a video game purchase. How much money is in her savings account after this purchase?

Step 1:	Step 2:
Choose your operation. Write the problem vertically, and line up the decimal points. $$\begin{array}{r} \$207.90 \\ -\$\ 42.79 \\ \hline \end{array}$$	Subtract and regroup as you normally would with whole numbers. Start in the place all the way to the right (in this case, the hundredths place). $$\begin{array}{r} {\scriptstyle 1\ 10 \qquad 8\ 10} \\ \$2\cancel{0}7.9\cancel{0} \\ -\$\ 42.79 \\ \hline \$165.11 \end{array}$$

PRACTICE: Now you try

Solve the following problems.

1. 45.083 – 2.67	2. 18.35 – 7.645
3. Phoebe's gymnastic team scored 190.275 points at their first meet. They scored 189.790 points at their second meet. What is the difference in scores between the two meets?	4. Ivan rode his bike 5.81 kilometers on Friday. He rode 7.205 kilometers on Saturday. How many more kilometers did he ride on Saturday than on Friday?
5. 78.558 – 1.782	6. 401.5 – 21.406
7. Mrs. Baez filled her gas tank with 18.605 gallons of gas. Her husband filled his gas tank with 1.25 gallons less. How many gallons does Mr. Baez' gas tank hold?	8. Caroline spent $18.28 at the Amazing Reads book store. She gave the cashier a twenty-dollar bill. How much change will she receive?

Standard: CCSS.Math.Content.6.NS.B.3

Evelyn subtracted 2.0 from 6.25 and got 6.05 as the answer. Is she correct? If not, where did she make her mistake? Show your work and write your explanation here.

ACE IT TIME!

	yes	no
Did you underline the question in the word problem?	○	○
Did you circle the numbers or number words?	○	○
Did you box the supporting details or information needed to solve the problem?	○	○
Did you draw a picture or a graphic organizer and write a math sentence to show your thinking?	○	○
Did you label your numbers and your picture?	○	○
Did you explain your thinking and use math vocabulary words in your explanation?	○	○

Math Vocabulary

decimal point place

hundredths place

subtract

value tenths place

MATH ON THE MOVE

Find a store circular or any advertisement that lists prices. Choose two items and subtract the prices. Which item costs more? How much more? Use subtraction to compare other prices.

Multiplying Decimals

UNPACK THE STANDARD
You will multiply decimals using the standard algorithm.

LEARN IT: To multiply decimals, follow the same rules as multiplying and dividing whole numbers. Use what you already know and apply the same strategies and methods. Remember to place the decimal point in your answer in the correct place!

Example: Use a model to find the product of 0.60 x 0.30.

Step 1:	**Step 2:**
Using a hundreds grid, shade in 0.60, or 0.6, vertically.	Next, shade in 0.30, or 0.3, horizontally.
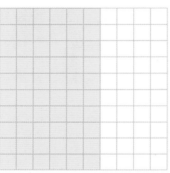	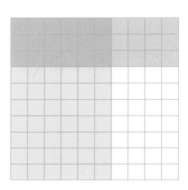

Step 3: Solve.
The answer is the part of the hundreds grid that is shaded twice. In this case, it is the green section!

think!
6 × 3 = 18!

$$0.60 \times 0.30 = 0.18$$

Example: Use the standard algorithm to find the product of 25.84 and 3.7.

Step 1:

Line up the numbers vertically and multiply as you would with whole numbers.

```
   2 5 . 8 4
 ×       3.7
 ─────────────
   1 8 8 8 8
 + 7 7 5 2 0
 ─────────────
   9 5 6 0 8
```

think! Ignore the decimal points until you get to the product at the end!

Step 2:

Count the decimal places in each factor. Add. Put the total number of decimal places in the product.

```
   2 5 . 8 4  ──→   2 decimal places
 ×       3.7  ──→ + 1 decimal place
 ───────────────────────────────────
   9 5.6 0 8  ──→   3 decimal places
```

$$25.84 \times 3.7 = 95.608$$

Standard: CCSS.Math.Content.6.NS.B.3

PRACTICE: Now you try

Multiply and divide the following decimals.

1. 4.35 × 2.7	2. 25.7 × 0.3	3. 8.15 × 7.84

4. Thomas bought 3.75 meters of rope. The rope cost $0.98 per meter. How much did he spend? *Hint:* Round your answer to the nearest hundredth.	5. Mr. Banderas bought 2.5 pounds of steak for the family barbeque. The steak cost $8.50 per pound. How much did he spend in all?

Viola bought 2.5 pounds of cherries at $1.99 per pound. She said she spent less than $5.00 on the cherries. Do you agree with her? Why or why not? Show your work and write your explanation here.

ACE IT TIME!

	yes	no
Did you underline the question in the word problem?	○	○
Did you circle the numbers or number words?	○	○
Did you box the supporting details or information needed to solve the problem?	○	○
Did you draw a picture or a graphic organizer and write a math sentence to show your thinking?	○	○
Did you label your numbers and your picture?	○	○
Did you explain your thinking and use math vocabulary words in your explanation?	○	○

Math Vocabulary

decimal place
decimal point
hundredths
multiply
thousandths

MATH ON THE MOVE

Go shopping! Pay attention to the decimals in the prices of things you buy (or would like to buy!) Many prices are shown in decimal form. What if you were to buy more than one of that item? Multiply the decimals to find the total cost!

Dividing Decimals

UNPACK THE STANDARD
You will divide decimals using the standard algorithm.

LEARN IT: To multiply and divide decimals, follow the same rules as multiplying and dividing whole numbers. Use what you already know and apply the same strategies and methods. Remember to place the decimal point in your answer in the correct place!

Example: 29.64 ÷ 0.24

Step 1:	Step 2:	Step 3:	Step 4:
Make the divisor a whole number by multiplying by powers of 10 (10, 100, or 1000). Multiply the dividend by the same amount.	Place the decimal point in the quotient above the spot it is in the dividend.	Divide as you would with whole numbers.	Place a 0 in the tenths place and continue dividing until there is no remainder. Repeat in the hundredths place if needed.

Step 1:
$0.24 \times 100 = 24$

$29.64 \times 100 = 2964$

think! Move the decimal of the divisor 2 places to the right to make it a whole number. Do the same for the dividend!

Step 2:
$$24\overline{)2964.}$$

Step 3:
$$\begin{array}{r} 123. \\ 24\overline{)2964.} \\ -24 \\ \hline 56 \\ -48 \\ \hline 84 \\ -72 \\ \hline 12 \end{array}$$

Step 4:
$$\begin{array}{r} 123.5 \\ 24\overline{)2964.0} \\ -24 \\ \hline 56 \\ -48 \\ \hline 84 \\ -72 \\ \hline 120 \\ -120 \\ \hline 0 \end{array}$$

$29.64 \div 0.24 = 123.5$

PRACTICE: Now you try

Solve the following problems.

1. 141.86 ÷ 8.2	2. 61.104 ÷ 13.4	3. 527.85 ÷ 15.3
4. Jaxon spent $18.00 going on rides at the county fair. Each ride cost $1.50. How many rides did he go on?		5. Miranda spent $32.83 on 9.8 gallons of gas for her scooter. How much did each gallon of gas cost?
6. 16.06 ÷ 0.08	7. 22.36 ÷ 2.6	8. 112.75 ÷ 5.5

Sasha babysat her cousin for 2.5 hours each day for 3 days. She earned a total of $41.25. How much did she earn per hour? Show your work and write your explanation here.

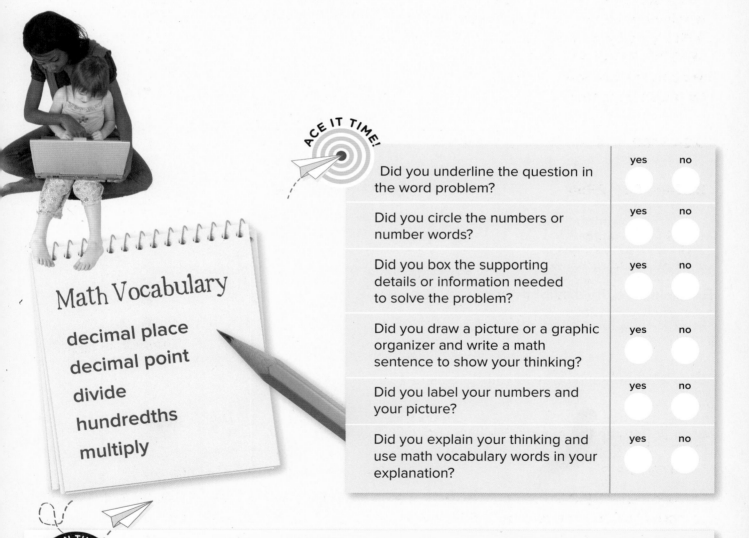

Math Vocabulary

decimal place

decimal point

divide

hundredths

multiply

ACE IT TIME!

	yes	no
Did you underline the question in the word problem?	○	○
Did you circle the numbers or number words?	○	○
Did you box the supporting details or information needed to solve the problem?	○	○
Did you draw a picture or a graphic organizer and write a math sentence to show your thinking?	○	○
Did you label your numbers and your picture?	○	○
Did you explain your thinking and use math vocabulary words in your explanation?	○	○

MATH ON THE MOVE

Helpful hint: You can use grid paper to help you write decimals in the correct place value when you add, subtract, multiply, or divide!

Greatest Common Factors

UNPACK THE STANDARD
You will find the greatest common factor of two whole numbers.

LEARN IT: *The Greatest Common Factor,* or *GCF,* is the greatest factor that two or more numbers have in common. Remember, a factor of a number can divide evenly into a given number. A factor times another factor equals a product!

Example: Find the GCF of 8 and 12.

Step 1:	**Step 2:**	**Step 3:**
List all of the factors of both numbers from least to greatest. 8: 1, 2, 4, 8 12: 1, 2, 3, 4, 6, 12	Underline the common factors of 8 and 12. 8: <u>1</u>, <u>2</u>, <u>4</u>, 8 12: <u>1</u>, <u>2</u>, 3, <u>4</u>, 6, 12	Circle the Greatest Common Factor. 8: 1, 2, ④, 8 12: 1, 2, 3, ④, 6, 12 The GCF of 8 and 12 is 4.
think! 1 × 8 = 8, so they are both factors of 8. 2 × 4 = 8, so they are also factors of 8. List them in order from least to greatest. Will every number have 1 as a factor?	**think!** Look for factors that you see listed for both numbers!	**think!** The GCF is the greatest factor both numbers have in common!

You can also use the GCF to help solve problems using the **Distributive Property.**

Example: Use the distributive property to solve 48 + 12

Step 1: Find the GCF of 48 and 12.

48: 1, 2, 3, 4, 6, 8, ⑫, 16, 24, 48
12: 1, 2, 3, 4, 6, ⑫   The GCF is 12

Step 2: Write each addend with 12 as a factor.

$48 = 12 \times 4$
$12 = 12 \times 1$

Step 3: Rewrite the expression as a sum with the factors, and solve using the distributive property.

$48 + 12 = (12 \times 4) + (12 \times 1)$
$(12 \times 4) + (12 \times 1) = 12 \times (4 + 1) = 12 \times (5) = 60$
$48 + 12 = 60$

think!
This may not be the fastest way to find the sum, but it helps you express the sum in a different way!

Standard: CCSS.Math.Content.6.NS.B.4

PRACTICE: Now you try

List the factors of each number. Find the GCF of each pair of numbers.

1. 9, 24	**2.** 14, 28	**3.** 16, 40
4. 15, 60	**5.** 25, 45	**6.** 36, 48

Use the distributive property to find each sum using the GCF.

7. 16 + 24	**8.** 50 + 75	**9.** 56 + 35

Tamara has 35 pencils and 28 erasers that she is putting into gift bags. Each bag will have the same number of pencils and erasers. What is the greatest number of bags Tamara can make with no pencils or erasers left over? How many pencils will be in each bag? How many erasers? *Hint:* Start with the GCF first! Show your work and explain your thinking on a piece of paper.

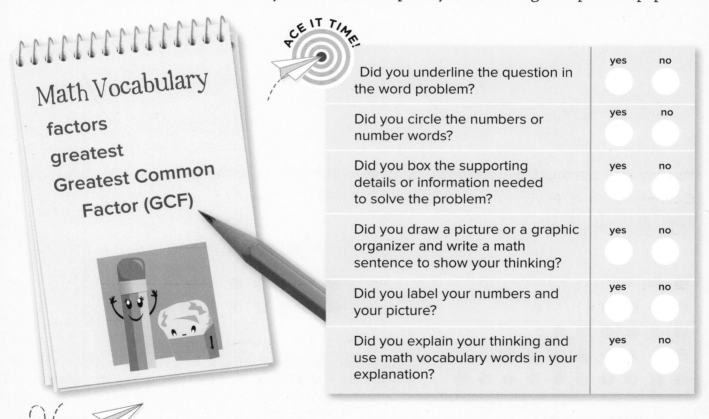

Math Vocabulary

factors
greatest
Greatest Common Factor (GCF)

ACE IT TIME!

	yes	no
Did you underline the question in the word problem?	◯	◯
Did you circle the numbers or number words?	◯	◯
Did you box the supporting details or information needed to solve the problem?	◯	◯
Did you draw a picture or a graphic organizer and write a math sentence to show your thinking?	◯	◯
Did you label your numbers and your picture?	◯	◯
Did you explain your thinking and use math vocabulary words in your explanation?	◯	◯

MATH ON THE MOVE

Flip the cards! Flip two number cards 1–9. List the factors of both numbers and find the GCF. Are there some numbers whose GCF is 1? Why is that? Now play again but flip four cards, to make 2 two-digit numbers!

Least Common Multiples

UNPACK THE STANDARD
You will find the least common multiple of two whole numbers.

LEARN IT: The *Least Common Multiple*, or *LCM,* is the least (or lowest) multiple that two or more numbers have in common. Remember, a *multiple* of a number is the product of that number and another factor.

Example: Find the LCM of 8 and 12.

Step 1:	Step 2:	Step 3:
List a few multiples of both numbers.	Underline the common multiples of 8 and 12.	Circle the least common multiple, or LCM.
8: 8, 16, 24, 32, 40, 48...	8: 8, 16, <u>24</u>, 32, 40, <u>48</u>...	8: 8, 16, 24, 32, 40, 48...
12: 12, 24, 36, 48, 60...	12: 12, <u>24</u>, 36, <u>48</u>, 60...	12: 12, 24, 36, 48, 60...
think! 8 × 1, 8 × 2, 8 × 3... You could keep going, but stopping after 4 or 5 multiples is usually enough!		**think!** 8 and 12 have at least two multiples in common, 24 and 48, but which one is the least, or lowest?
		The LCM of 8 and 12 is 24.

You can use counters to model the least common multiple of two numbers. Look at the example below to show how to find the LCM of 2 and 5 using counters.

Example: Find the LCM of 2 and 5.

Multiples of 2:

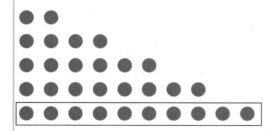

Multiples of 5:

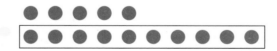

think! Can you explain how this model shows the least common multiple of 2 and 5? What if you had more counters and kept showing more multiples? What would be the next common multiple of these two numbers?

PRACTICE: Now you try

Find the LCM of each pair of numbers.

1. 6, 8	**2.** 2, 5	**3.** 4, 9
4. 9 and 12	**5.** 10 and 12	**6.** 8 and 3

7. Hot dogs are sold in packages of 10. Hot dog buns are sold in packages of 8. What is the least number of hot dogs and buns you can buy to have an equal number of hot dogs and buns for your family cookout?	**8.** At the fruit stand, apples come in bags of 4. Oranges come in bags of 6. What is the least number of bags of apples and oranges you can buy to have an equal number of each fruit?

Ezra says that another way to find the least common multiple of two numbers is to multiply the two numbers together. Is he correct? Try Ezra's method by finding the LCM of 5 and 6. Now see if it works for other numbers, such as 5 and 10. Does this method find the LCM every time? Can you explain Ezra's thinking? Show your work and explain your thinking on a piece of paper.

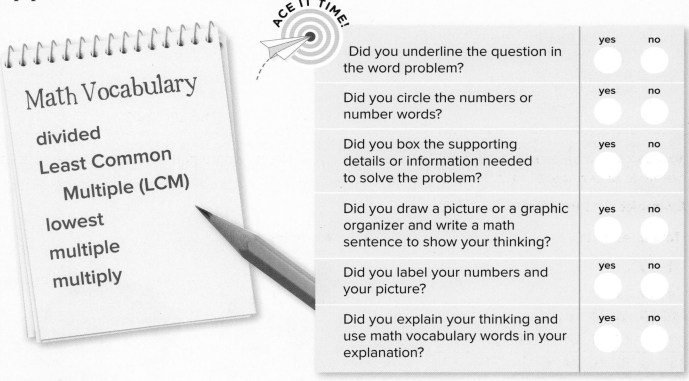

Math Vocabulary

divided

Least Common
   Multiple (LCM)

lowest

multiple

multiply

ACE IT TIME!

	yes	no
Did you underline the question in the word problem?	○	○
Did you circle the numbers or number words?	○	○
Did you box the supporting details or information needed to solve the problem?	○	○
Did you draw a picture or a graphic organizer and write a math sentence to show your thinking?	○	○
Did you label your numbers and your picture?	○	○
Did you explain your thinking and use math vocabulary words in your explanation?	○	○

Think About It: You are only asked to find the GCF of numbers less than or equal to 100, and the LCM of numbers less than or equal to 12. Why do you think this is the given limit? Why do you think we are able to find a greatest common factor, but not a greatest common multiple?

REVIEW

Congratulations! You've finished the lessons for this unit. This means you have reviewed division of whole numbers. You can add, subtract, multiply, and divide decimals! You've also learned the difference between the Greatest Common Factor (GCF) and Least Common Multiple (LCM).

Now it's time to prove your skills with number system operations. Solve the problems below! Use all of the methods you have learned.

Activity Section 1: Division Review

Solve the following problems.

1. 4,825 ÷ 32	2. 2,414 ÷ 120	3. 42,548 ÷ 128

4. The library at Shakespeare Middle School has 3,325 books. If each bookshelf can hold 92 books, how many bookshelves does the library need?

5. The Longwood County school district has $37,310 to spend on new technology for the schools. The district is going to provide one new tablet for each middle school classroom in the district. Each tablet costs $455. For how many middle school classrooms can the district afford to buy a tablet?

Standard: CCSS.Math.Content.6.NS.B.2, 6.NS.B.3, 6.NS.B.4

Activity Section 2: Adding Decimals

Solve the following problems.

1. 125.78 + 6.3	2. 51.06 + 335.789	3. 645.589 + 42.11

4. Zak collected data for his chemistry class. The first beaker he measured had 3.55 mL of liquids. The second beaker had 1.75 more mL than the first beaker. How many milliliters of liquid did he measure in all?

5. Xavier ran 3.5 kilometers from his house to the park and another 2.45 kilometers through the park before turning around and running back home. How many kilometers did he run in all?

Activity Section 3: Subtracting Decimals

Solve the following problems.

1. 88.445 − 24.75	2. 456.07 − 55.68	3. 600.2 − 19.23

4. Giada had $35.59 in her bank account. She spent $6.95 downloading music. How much money did she have left in her bank account?

5. Kyla spent $3.48 on snacks at the concession stand. She paid with a ten-dollar bill. How much change will she receive?

Activity Section 4: Multiplying Decimals

Solve the following problems.

1. 23.48 × 12.3	2. 7.24 × 0.35	3. 478.5 × 25.6

4. Rob jumped 1.32 meters high on the high jump. The record for the highest jump at his school is 1.5 times that. How high is the record high jump at Rob's school?

5. The easy hiking trail in Mountain Bluffs is 4.75 miles long. Katy hiked half (or 0.5) of the trail and then stopped for a break. How many miles did she hike before she stopped for her break?

Activity Section 5: Dividing Decimals

Solve the following problems.

1. 48.23 ÷ 0.35	2. 809.6 ÷ 2.3	3. 210.12 ÷ 15.45

4. Leanne spent $9.90 downloading songs that cost $1.98 each. How many songs did she download?

5. Samara earned $18.15 for working 3.3 hours at the Scoop It ice cream shop. How much does she make per hour?

Standard: CCSS.Math.Content.6.NS.B.2, 6.NS.B.3, 6.NS.B.4

Activity Section 6: Greatest Common Factors

List the factors of each number and find the GCF.

1. 8 and 28 8: 28: GCF =	**2.** 5 and 20 5: 20: GCF =	**3.** 16 and 32 16: 32: GCF =
4. 12 and 72 12: 72: GCF =	**5.** 18 and 45 18: 45: GCF =	**6.** 20 and 60 20: 60: GCF =

Use the distributive property to solve the sum.

7. 30 + 45	**8.** 12 + 36	**9.** 36 + 27

Activity Section 7: Least Common Multiples

List several multiples of each number until you find the LCM.

1. 8 and 12 8: 12: LCM =	**2.** 2 and 7 2: 7: LCM =	**3.** 9 and 6 9: 6: LCM =
4. 2 and 20 2: 20: LCM =	**5.** 5 and 10 5: 10: LCM =	**6.** 3 and 4 3: 4: LCM =

UNDERSTAND

Understand the meaning of what you have learned and apply your knowledge.

Use what you know about factors and multiples to find the GCF (Greatest Common Factor) and LCM (Least Common Multiple) of two numbers. Use your number sense to help look for patterns between two or more numbers.

Activity Section

Solve these riddles!

1. The LCM of two numbers less than or equal to 12 is ten more than five. What are the two numbers?

2. The GCF of three numbers less than or equal to 12 is 2. Their LCM is 12. What are the three numbers?

3. The GCF of two numbers less than 100 is 5. One of the numbers is a multiple of 10. Their LCM is 30. What are the two numbers?

4. Write your own GCF riddle.

5. Write your own LCM riddle.

Standard: CCSS.Math.Content.6.NS.B.4, CCSS.Math.Practice.MP1, MP2, MP4, MP6, MP7, MP8

DISCOVER

Discover how you can apply the information you have learned.

One of the most common ways you use multiplication and division of decimals is when working with money. Shopping and looking for "the better deal" is a very common real-world application.

Activity Section

Coral buys 5 T-shirts at The Closet for the same amount that Wear It sells 4 T-shirts. If one T-shirt costs $9.80 at Wear It, how much does one T-shirt cost at The Closet? Her friend Jasmine thinks Wear It offers a better deal, but Coral thinks The Closet does. Who do you agree with and why?

CORE Rational Number Concepts

Understanding Integers

UNPACK THE STANDARD
You will use positive and negative numbers to describe real-life situations.

LEARN IT: A *positive number* is greater than zero. A *negative number* is less than zero. *Integers* are positive and negative whole numbers without fractional parts or decimals. You can find integers on a number line. Zero is also an integer!

Integers represent values on the number line.

Positive integers are to the right of 0, and negative integers are to the left.

Let's discuss what these negative numbers represent. To answer this, you have to know what zero means. This depends on the situation.

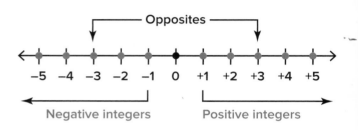

Example: A football team gained 25 yards on a play. In the next play, they lost 5 yards. How do you represent these situations using integers?

Step 1:	**Step 2:**
Decide what 0 means in this situation.	Identify what is happening in the situation.
Here, 0 is where the football starts on the field before the play begins. 	In the first play, the team gained 25 yards. A gain is a positive action, so a gain of 25 yards is written as +25. In the next play, the team lost 5 yards. A loss is a negative action, so a loss of 5 yards is written as −5.

PRACTICE: Now you try

Write the opposite of each integer.

1. +8	2. −17	3. +54	4. −104

Standard: CCSS.Math.Content.6.NS.C.5

Name the integer that represents the situation.

5. Morgan deposited $40 into her bank account. _____

6. Joleen's dog lost 2 pounds. _____

7. The temperature dropped 13 degrees overnight. _____

8. Denver, Colorado, is exactly 1 mile above sea level. _____

9. New Orleans, Louisiana, is about 7 feet below sea level. _____

10. Anthony lost 15 points in a card game. _____

Micah's score in his video game decreased by 5,000 points from one level to the next. He writes this integer as +5,000. Do you agree with him? Why or why not? Show your work and write your explanation here.

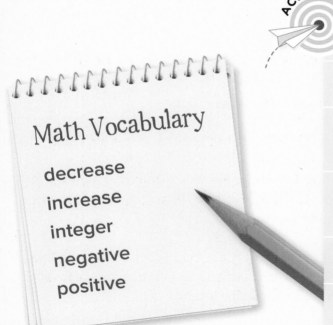

ACE IT TIME!

Math Vocabulary

decrease

increase

integer

negative

positive

	yes	no
Did you underline the question in the word problem?	○	○
Did you circle the numbers or number words?	○	○
Did you box the supporting details or information needed to solve the problem?	○	○
Did you draw a picture or a graphic organizer and write a math sentence to show your thinking?	○	○
Did you label your numbers and your picture?	○	○
Did you explain your thinking and use math vocabulary words in your explanation?	○	○

MATH ON THE MOVE

Look for places in real life where you can express numbers as positive and negative integers. Remember, whether a number is positive or negative depends on the situation!

Graphing Integers on a Number Line

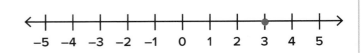

UNPACK THE STANDARD
You will graph integers and their opposites on a number line.

LEARN IT: You can best see the relationship between a positive and a negative number on a number line.

Example: Use a number line to find 3 and −3.

Step 1:

Graph 3 on the number line.

3, or +3, is 3 hops to the right of 0 on a number line.

Step 2:

Graph the opposite of 3, or −3, on the number line.

−3 is 3 hops to the left of 0 on a number line.

think! Does 0 have an opposite?

Step 3:

Observe.

See how they are equal distances from zero but on opposite sides.

You can even write the opposite of the opposite of a number. You show this with parentheses.

Example: −(−3), or the opposite of the opposite of 3, equals 3.

Notice that the opposite of the opposite of an integer is the integer itself!

PRACTICE: Now you try

Find the opposite of each integer. Graph both on the number line.

1. +4 Opposite integer = _____

2. −7 Opposite integer = _____

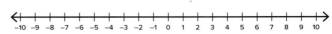

3. −9 Opposite integer = _____

4. +2 Opposite integer = _____

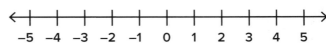

Standards: CCSS.Math.Content.6.NS.C.6a, and 6.NS,C.6c

Write the value of each integer.

5. −(−14)	**6.** Opposite of the opposite of 48	**7.** −(−5)
8. Opposite of the opposite of −105	**9.** −(15)	**10.** −(−1)

Jenna plotted points on the number line shown below. Identify the integer that each point represents. Plot the opposite of each integer on the number line, and label them points E, F, G, and H.

A =

B =

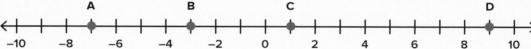

C =

D =

E =

F =

G =

H =

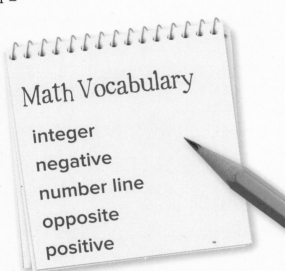

Math Vocabulary

integer

negative

number line

opposite

positive

ACE IT TIME!

	yes	no
Did you underline the question in the word problem?	○	○
Did you circle the numbers or number words?	○	○
Did you box the supporting details or information needed to solve the problem?	○	○
Did you draw a picture or a graphic organizer and write a math sentence to show your thinking?	○	○
Did you label your numbers and your picture?	○	○
Did you explain your thinking and use math vocabulary words in your explanation?	○	○

MATH ON THE MOVE

Talk about it! How can you use a number line to find the opposite of a number? Why are number lines a valuable tool in math? When would a vertical number line be helpful when working with integers?

Comparing and Ordering Integers

UNPACK THE STANDARD
You will compare and order integers.

LEARN IT: You know that a negative number is less than zero. This means negative numbers are also less than positive numbers. You can order positive numbers because you know that 7 is more than 3. 7 is farther to the right on a number line. Does this mean −7 is more than −3?.

Think about positive numbers on a number line. As you move to the right, numbers become greater. As you move to the left, numbers become lesser. The same is true of negative numbers. Let's model the problem.

Example: Which is greater: −3 or −7?

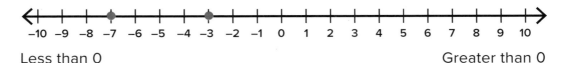

Less than 0   Greater than 0

Step 1:	Step 2:
Plot both integers on the number line.	Observe. −7 is farther to the left. It is farther away from 0. This means −7 is less than −3.
	You can write this as an ***inequality statement:***
	−3 > −7

You can also show this with a vertical number line. The farther up a number is, the greater it is. The farther down a number is, the less it is.

Example: Which has a lesser value: −1 or −3?

Step 1:	Step 2:
Plot both integers on the number line.	Observe. −3 is farther down on the number line.
	−3 < −1

PRACTICE: Now you try

Plot each integer on the number line. Compare the integers. Write a > or < symbol in the circle.

1. −8 ◯ −4

←|—|—|—|—|—|—|—|—|—|—|—|—|—|—|—|—|—|—|—|—|→
−10 −9 −8 −7 −6 −5 −4 −3 −2 −1 0 1 2 3 4 5 6 7 8 9 10

2. −1 ◯ −2

←|—|—|—|—|—|—|—|—|—|—|—|—|—|—|—|—|—|—|—|—|→
−10 −9 −8 −7 −6 −5 −4 −3 −2 −1 0 1 2 3 4 5 6 7 8 9 10

Standard: CCSS.Math.Content.6.NS.C.7a and 6.NS.C.6c

Compare these integers without a number line. Write a > or < symbol in the circle. Think of each integer's distance from zero.

3. −6 ◯ −7	4. −8 ◯ −7	5. 0 ◯ −3

List the integers in order from *least to greatest.*

6. −12, −15, −13, −14	7. 1, −2, −1, 2	8. −11, −5, −7 , −17

```
+10
 0
−10
−20
−30
−40
−50
−60
−70
−80
−90
```

The two coldest temperatures on record in the United States are −80 degrees Fahrenheit in Alaska on January 23, 1971, and −70 degrees Fahrenheit in Montana on January 20, 1954. Which is the colder temperature? How do you know? *Hint:* Think of the vertical number line as a thermometer! Show your work and explain your thinking on a piece of paper.

ACE IT TIME!

	yes	no
Did you underline the question in the word problem?	◯	◯
Did you circle the numbers or number words?	◯	◯
Did you box the supporting details or information needed to solve the problem?	◯	◯
Did you draw a picture or a graphic organizer and write a math sentence to show your thinking?	◯	◯
Did you label your numbers and your picture?	◯	◯
Did you explain your thinking and use math vocabulary words in your explanation?	◯	◯

Math Vocabulary

inequality statement

integer

negative

MATH ON THE MOVE

Flip the cards! Use number cards 1–9 to compare negative integers. For example, you flip a 4 and 5. Find the opposite value of each card (−4 and −5) and compare. What inequality statement can you write?

Ordering Rational Numbers

UNPACK THE STANDARD
You will order rational numbers on a number line.

LEARN IT: Decimals, fractions, and integers are all ***rational numbers.*** Rational numbers can be made by dividing one integer by another nonzero integer. Remember that dividing can be shown as a fraction or ratio. The word "rational" actually comes from "ratio!"

You can plot rational numbers on a number line.

Example: Compare −0.3 and −0.8.

> **think!** 0.3 Can also be written as $\frac{3}{10}$. Remember that 1 whole can be written as $\frac{10}{10}$. Since you only have 3 out of 10, the fraction is a ratio of parts to the whole!

Step 1:	**Step 2:**
Plot each number on a number line. Remember that tenths are between 0 and 1. So the opposite (negative) is between 0 and −1.	Compare. Write a > or < symbol to show the inequality. $$-0.3 > -0.8$$
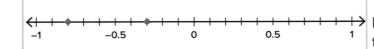	Remember, the closer a negative number gets to zero, the greater its value!

Fractions are also rational numbers. They can be plotted on a number line.

Example: Compare $-\frac{4}{5}$ and $-\frac{2}{10}$.

Step 1:	**Step 2:**	**Step 3:**
Rewrite the fractions using common denominators. $$-\frac{2}{10} = -\frac{1}{5}$$ **think!** You could also convert $\frac{4}{5}$ into tenths, but drawing a number line in tenths means drawing more sections!	Plot each rational number on a number line. Break the number line up based on the common denominator. 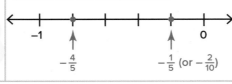	Compare. $$-\frac{4}{5} < -\frac{2}{10}$$

PRACTICE: Now you try

Plot each rational number. Compare using > or <.

> **think!** Convert the fraction to a decimal!

1. $-\frac{3}{4}$ ◯ $-\frac{1}{2}$

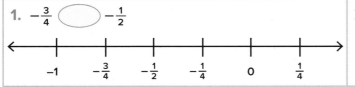

2. $-.25$ ◯ $-\frac{2}{4}$

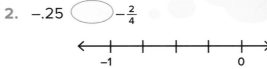

Standard: CCSS.Math.Content.6.NS.C.7b

Compare using > or <.

3. −8°F ◯ −8.5°F	**4.** −1$\frac{2}{10}$ points ◯ −1.4 points
5. −$2.58 ◯ −$2.50	**6.** −4.5°C ◯ −4.25°C
7. −36$\frac{1}{4}$ feet below sea level ◯ −36.5 feet below sea level	**8.** −2$\frac{3}{4}$ meter ◯ −2.20 meter

Mount Everest, located in Nepal, is the tallest mountain in the world. Temperatures at the top of the summit can reach −60.24°C. Other Mt. Everest summit temperatures have been recorded at −36$\frac{1}{4}$°C, −36.8°C, and −45.25°C. List these temperatures in order from least to greatest, or from coldest to "warmest!" Show your work and write your explanation here.

ACE IT TIME!

	yes	no
Did you underline the question in the word problem?	◯	◯
Did you circle the numbers or number words?	◯	◯
Did you box the supporting details or information needed to solve the problem?	◯	◯
Did you draw a picture or a graphic organizer and write a math sentence to show your thinking?	◯	◯
Did you label your numbers and your picture?	◯	◯
Did you explain your thinking and use math vocabulary words in your explanation?	◯	◯

Math Vocabulary

decimal

fraction

negative numbers

rational numbers

MATH ON THE MOVE

Did you know there is such thing as an irrational number? Irrational numbers are numbers that cannot be written as a fraction, or a ratio. One famous irrational number is called Pi (or π =3.14159...). Do some research online with an adult to find out why Pi is considered an irrational number. Check out this website: *http://www.mathsisfun.com/irrational-numbers.html*.

Understanding Absolute Value

UNPACK THE STANDARD
You will find the absolute value of a rational number.

LEARN IT: The *absolute value* of a rational number is that number's distance from 0 on the number line.

The absolute value of −3 is written as |−3| = 3.

It is 3 units away from 0.

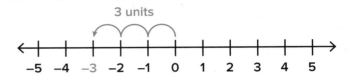

Example: Find two integers on the number line that have an absolute value of 6. Plot them on a number line.

Since absolute value measures distance from 0, both numbers have to be 6 units from 0. The numbers can be to the right or left of zero.

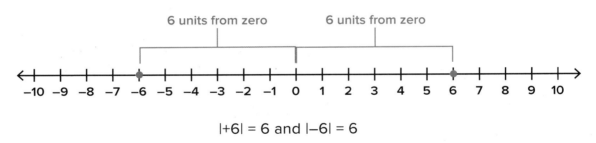

|+6| = 6 and |−6| = 6

You can also find the absolute value of fractions and decimals.

Example: Find the absolute value of −1.35.   −1.35 is 1.35 units to the left of 0. |−1.35| = 1.35

Example: Find the absolute value of $4\frac{3}{4}$. $4\frac{3}{4}$ is $4\frac{3}{4}$ units to the right of 0. $|4\frac{3}{4}| = 4\frac{3}{4}$

PRACTICE: Now you try

Find the absolute value.

1. |−44| =	2. |−81| =	3. $|7\frac{3}{5}|$ =
4. |20.5|	5. $|-3\frac{1}{3}|$ =	6. |−45.25| =

Standard: CCSS.Math.Content.6.NS.C.7c

Use absolute values to describe these real-world situations.

7. A bank account balance of −$25.50 = a debt of _____ . *Hint:* A debt is money owed!	**8.** A submarine at −32 feet = _____ feet below sea level.	**9.** An airplane flying at 42,000 feet = _____ feet above sea level.

Nora and Juan answered the same problem in math class: Which is the greater debt, −$40 or −$45? Nora answered that −$40 is a greater debt because it is closer to zero. Juan answered −$45 is a greater debt because it is farther from zero. Who do you agree with and why? Use what you have learned about absolute value to explain. Show your work and explain your thinking on a piece of paper.

Math Vocabulary

absolute value

debt

integer

negative integer

zero

ACE IT TIME!

	yes	no
Did you underline the question in the word problem?	○	○
Did you circle the numbers or number words?	○	○
Did you box the supporting details or information needed to solve the problem?	○	○
Did you draw a picture or a graphic organizer and write a math sentence to show your thinking?	○	○
Did you label your numbers and your picture?	○	○
Did you explain your thinking and use math vocabulary words in your explanation?	○	○

MATH ON THE MOVE

Think about it! Can the absolute value of a number ever be negative? *Hint:* Can you ever measure a negative distance? When you use a ruler, can you measure less than 0 inches?

Comparing With and Without Absolute Value

UNPACK THE STANDARD
You will correctly use number order and absolute value in real-world situations.

LEARN IT: You know that ordering numbers means stating which numbers are greater or less than others. Numbers increase in value as you move to the right on a number line and decrease as you move to the left. You also know that absolute value measures a number's distance from zero. Absolute value increases as you move away from zero—to the right and the left!

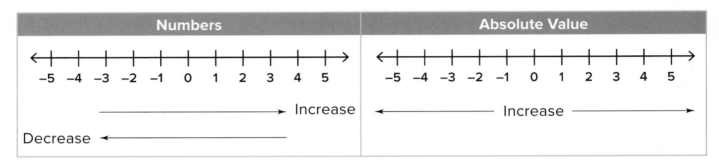

Numbers	Absolute Value

Some real-world situations use number order to solve. Some use absolute value. It depends on the situation.

Example: Jeremy is scuba diving at −24 feet. Julia is diving at −28 feet. Who is diving deeper below the surface?

Step 1:	Step 2:
Decide whether to order the numbers or compare absolute values.	Find the absolute values.

Step 2:

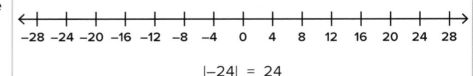

$$|-24| = 24$$

$$|-28| = 28$$

Jeremy is diving at **24 feet** below the surface.
Julia is diving at **28 feet** below the surface.

Step 1:

Decide whether to order the numbers or compare absolute values.

The deeper diver will be the furthest from sea level. The sea level is at 0 feet below the surface. This means the deeper diver will have the value furthest from 0.

Step 3:

Compare absolute values. $|-24| < |-28|$ $24 < 28$

Julia is deeper below the surface.

Standard: CCSS.Math.Content.6.NS.C.7d

PRACTICE: Now you try

Answer the following questions.

1. Carmen has an account balance of −$5. Does she have more or less than $3 of debt?	2. A football team lost 15 yards on their first play. Their last play was for −10 yards. On which play did they lose more yards?
3. Morgan, Tracy, and Greg all have lost points while playing a video game. Morgan has a score of −5 points. Tracy has a score of −2 points. Greg has a score of −10 points. Who has the lowest score?	4. The depth of Lake Michigan is −278 feet below the surface at its deepest point. Lake Erie has a depth of −210 feet. Which lake is shallower?

List any three numbers greater than |−24|. Explain how you know.

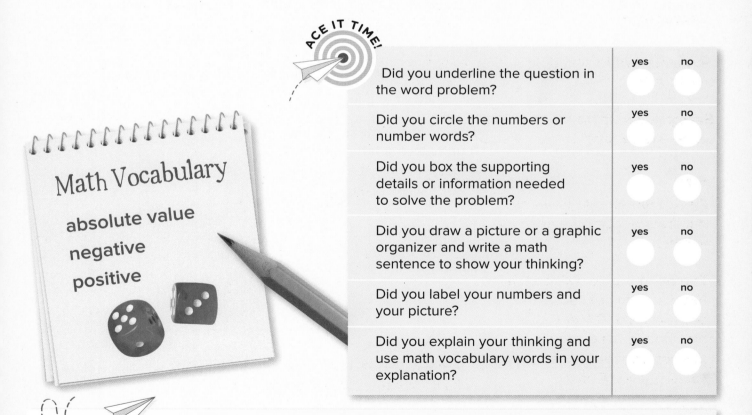

ACE IT TIME!

Math Vocabulary

absolute value

negative

positive

	yes	no
Did you underline the question in the word problem?		
Did you circle the numbers or number words?		
Did you box the supporting details or information needed to solve the problem?		
Did you draw a picture or a graphic organizer and write a math sentence to show your thinking?		
Did you label your numbers and your picture?		
Did you explain your thinking and use math vocabulary words in your explanation?		

MATH ON THE MOVE

Roll the dice! Roll four dice to make 2 two-digit numbers. Make them negative numbers. Order the numbers. Find and order their absolute values. Are the orders the same? Why or why not?

Ordered Pairs on a Coordinate Plane

UNPACK THE STANDARD
You will graph integers on a coordinate plane.

LEARN IT: Think about what you know about coordinate planes. You've graphed numbers on an *x*-axis and *y*-axis. The *x*-axis is horizontal. The *y*-axis is vertical. Ordered pairs (*x*, *y*) tell you where to plot the point.

However, before now you've only graphed in one quadrant, where *x* and *y* integers are positive.

There are 4 possible **quadrants** on a coordinate plane. The *x*-axis and *y*-axis can both be negative, too. The four quadrants are shown in the coordinate plane. Notice how quadrants II, III, and IV contain negative integers. The point at (0, 0) is called the origin.

Example: Plot (−3, −4) on a coordinate plane. In which quadrant is the point located?

Step 1:	Step 2:	Step 3:
Identify the quadrants on a coordinate plane. 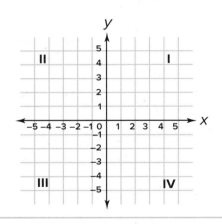	Plot (−3, −4) on the coordinate plane. The *x*-coordinate is −3. It is **3 units to the left** on the *x*-axis, starting at the origin (0, 0). The *y*-coordinate is −4. It is **4 units down** on the *y*-axis, starting at the origin (0, 0).	Identify the quadrant. The coordinate point (−3, −4) is located in quadrant III. 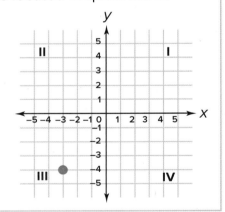

How does the point (−3, −4) relate to these points: (3, 4), (−3, 4), and (3, −4)?

When ordered pairs have the same numbers but different signs, they are opposite each other on the coordinate plane. The points (3, 4) and (−3, 4) differ in the sign of the 3. This sign changes the location on the *x*-axis. The *y*-axis points are the same, so the points are across from each other on the *y*-axis. They are called reflections across the *y*-axis!

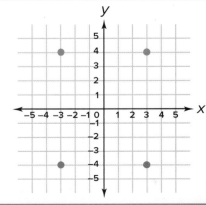

Standard: CCSS.Math.Content.6.NS.C.6b

PRACTICE: Now you try

Identify which quadrant each coordinate point is located in.

1. (3, 8) Quadrant: _____	2. (−4, 2) Quadrant: _____	3. (6, −3) Quadrant: _____	4. (−1, −1) Quadrant: _____

Each pair of coordinate points is a reflection across the x- or y-axis. Identify the axis.

5. (−8, −9) and (8, −9) Axis: _____	6. (−11, −12) and (−11, 12) Axis: _____

Plot and label each coordinate point on the plane.

7. A (−2, 4)

8. B (3, 2)

9. C (−4, 6)

10. D (−5, −2)

11. E (1, −3)

12. F (−6, −6)

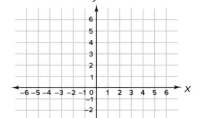

Jonah graphed the ordered pair (4, −4) and said it was located in quadrant III. Is he correct? Why or why not? Draw a coordinate plane on a piece of paper to help you explain your answer.

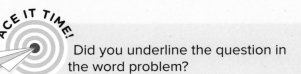

Math Vocabulary

coordinate grid

ordered pair

quadrant

x- and y-axes

x- and y-coordinates

ACE IT TIME!

	yes	no
Did you underline the question in the word problem?		
Did you circle the numbers or number words?		
Did you box the supporting details or information needed to solve the problem?		
Did you draw a picture or a graphic organizer and write a math sentence to show your thinking?		
Did you label your numbers and your picture?		
Did you explain your thinking and use math vocabulary words in your explanation?		

MATH ON THE MOVE Use sidewalk chalk to draw a large coordinate plane on the sidewalk outside. Be sure to label the x- and y-axes. With a friend or adult, take turns calling out ordered pairs (with positive and negative numbers) and walking to that spot. Tell which quadrant you are standing in!

Graphing Integers and Rational Numbers

UNPACK THE STANDARD
You will graph ordered pairs of rational numbers on a coordinate plane.

LEARN IT: You can graph all rational numbers the same way you graph integers. Remember, a rational number is any number that can be made by dividing one integer by another nonzero integer. Rational numbers include integers, fractions, and decimals.

Example: Plot the ordered pair $(-\frac{1}{2}, 1\frac{1}{2})$

Pay close attention to the number scale used on the *x*- and *y*-axes.

think!
$\frac{1}{2}$ is between 0 and 1, so
$-\frac{1}{2}$ is between 0 and –1.
$1\frac{1}{2}$ is between 1
and 2.

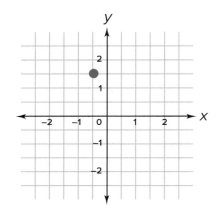

PRACTICE: Now you try

Plot and label the points on the coordinate plane.

1. A (2, 1)	**2.** B $(-1, -\frac{1}{2})$
3. C (–1.5, –1.5)	**4.** D (0, –2)
5. E (–2, 1.5)	**6.** F $(2\frac{1}{2}, -2\frac{1}{2})$
7. G $(1, -1\frac{1}{2})$	**8.** H (–0.5, 0.5)

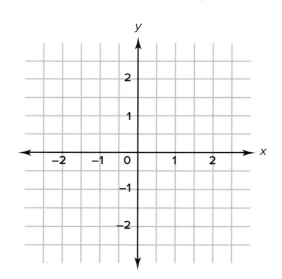

Create your own ordered pairs and plot them on the coordinate plane.

9. I (_____ , _____)	**10.** J (_____ , _____)
11. K (_____ , _____)	**12.** L (_____ , _____)

Standard: Standard: CCSS.Math.Content.6.NS.C.6c

Lena draws four points on a coordinate plane. She connects the points to form a rectangle. Point A is located at $(-3\frac{1}{2}, 2\frac{1}{2})$, point B is at $(3\frac{1}{2}, 2\frac{1}{2})$, and point C is at $(-3\frac{1}{2}, -1\frac{1}{2})$. Where is point D located? How do you know? Draw the coordinate grid to help you. Show your work and explain your thinking on a piece of paper.

ACE IT TIME!

Math Vocabulary

coordinate plane
ordered pair
rational numbers
x- and y-axes
x- and y-coordinates

	yes	no
Did you underline the question in the word problem?	○	○
Did you circle the numbers or number words?	○	○
Did you box the supporting details or information needed to solve the problem?	○	○
Did you draw a picture or a graphic organizer and write a math sentence to show your thinking?	○	○
Did you label your numbers and your picture?	○	○
Did you explain your thinking and use math vocabulary words in your explanation?	○	○

MATH ON THE MOVE

Graph paper is an excellent resource for drawing coordinate grids and plotting ordered pairs. Think of ways you can number the x- and y-axes to include even more rational numbers. For example, draw a coordinate plane labeled with the rational numbers 0.25, 0.50, 0.75, 1.0, 1.25, 1.50, and so on. Don't forget the negative numbers on quadrants II, III, and IV! Write some ordered pairs and plot them on the coordinate plane.

Graphing and Finding Distance on Coordinate Planes

UNPACK THE STANDARD
You will find the distance between two points on a coordinate plane.

LEARN IT: Now that you know how to graph coordinate pairs on a coordinate plane, let's find the distance between two points. Finding the distance can be as simple as counting the units between the points. You can also use absolute value to calculate distance.

Example: A map of Kendall's neighborhood is shown on the coordinate plane below. Each unit represents one block. Her house is located at the coordinate (−3, 2), and her friend Cori's house is located at (4, 2). What is the distance between Kendall's house and Cori's house?

A. Count the units. Since both points are on the same line in the coordinate plane, you can treat it like a number line.

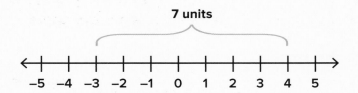

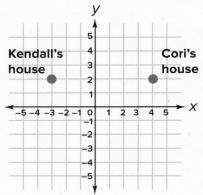

Since each unit equals 1 block, and the houses are 7 units apart, that means the houses are 7 blocks apart.

B. Use the absolute value to find the distance between the two points.

Look at the points (−3, 2) and (4, 2). They have different *x*-coordinates but the same *y*-coordinate. The distance between the different points is the answer. Find the distance by adding the absolute values.

Total distance = distance of point 1 from 0 + distance of point 2 from 0

Total distance = $|-3| + |4| = 3 + 4 = 7$

think! If the points are in the same quadrant, will you use addition or subtraction? Draw an example on the coordinate grid to find out. Use counting to check.

Standard: CCSS.Math.Content.6.NS.C.8

PRACTICE: Now you try

Use the coordinate plane to plot and label each set of ordered pairs. Find the distance between the points.

1. A (2, −1) and B (1, −1)

   Distance:

2. C (−3, 2) and D (−3, −3)

   Distance:

3. E (4, 4) and F (4, −3)

   Distance:

4. G (−2, −2) and H (3, −2)

   Distance:

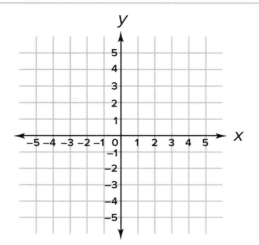

Rafi says the distance between the two points (2, −6) and (−6, −6) is four units. Do you agree with him? Why or why not? Show your work and explain your thinking on a piece of paper.

ACE IT TIME!

Math Vocabulary

absolute value

coordinate plane

x- and y-axes

x- and y-coordinates

	yes	no
Did you underline the question in the word problem?	○	○
Did you circle the numbers or number words?	○	○
Did you box the supporting details or information needed to solve the problem?	○	○
Did you draw a picture or a graphic organizer and write a math sentence to show your thinking?	○	○
Did you label your numbers and your picture?	○	○
Did you explain your thinking and use math vocabulary words in your explanation?	○	○

MATH ON THE MOVE

Talk about it! Why do you find the absolute value of coordinates when you are looking to find the distance between two points?

 REVIEW

Stop and think about what you have learned.

Congratulations! You've finished the lessons for this unit. This means you've learned about rational numbers and integers, how to graph ordered pairs, about absolute value and how to find the distance between two points on a coordinate plane.

Now it's time to prove your skills with rational numbers. Solve the problems below! Use all of the methods you have learned.

Activity Section 1: Understanding Integers

Write the opposite of each integer.

1. −44	2. +3	3. −121	4. 18

Name the integer that represents the situation.

5. Corbin's father lost 3 pounds. _____

6. Aliyah deposited $15 into her bank account. _____

7. Ben scored 500 points in a video game. _____

8. A football team gained 40 yards. _____

9. There was a $23.00 withdrawal from your bank account. _____

10. The temperature dropped 20 degrees. _____

Activity Section 2: Graphing Integers on a Number Line

Name the opposite integer. Graph both on the number line.

1. +1 Opposite integer =

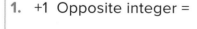

2. −9 Opposite integer =

3. −6 Opposite integer =

4. +2 Opposite integer =

Standard: CCSS.Math.Content.6.NS.C.5, 6.NS.C.6a-c, 6.NS.C.7a-d, 6.NS.C.8

Write the value of each integer.

5. −(−23)	**6.** Opposite of the opposite of 17	**7.** −(−8)
8. Opposite of the opposite of −45	**9.** − (34)	**10.** −(−11)

Activity Section 3: Comparing and Ordering Integers

Graph the integers on the number line and write > or < to compare.

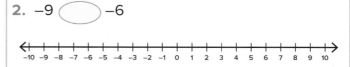

1. − 6 ⬭ −7

2. −9 ⬭ −6

Compare these integers. Write > or <.

3. −10 ⬭ −100	**4.** −33 ⬭ −36	**5.** −103 ⬭ −102

List the integers in order from *greatest* to *least*.

6. −22, −12, −21, −2 _____

7. 3, −3, −4, 4 _____

8. −88, −90, −86, −89 _____

Activity Section 4: Ordering Rational Numbers

Graph the rational numbers on the number line and write > or < to compare.

1. −0.25 ⬭ $-\frac{1}{2}$

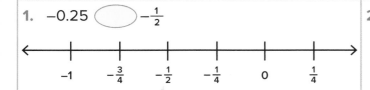

2. −0.75 ⬭ −0.50

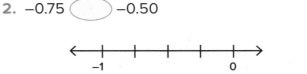

Compare. Write the rational numbers in order from *least* to *greatest*.

3. −2.5, −2.35, −2.25, −2.40 _____

4. $-\frac{1}{2}$, $-\frac{1}{4}$, −1, $-\frac{3}{4}$ _____

5. −3.20, $-3\frac{1}{4}$, −3.15, $-3\frac{1}{2}$ _____

6. −1.75, $-1\frac{1}{4}$, −1.5, $-1\frac{1}{5}$ _____

Activity Section 5: Understanding Absolute Value

Fill in the blanks.

1. $|-14| = $ _____	2. $|-72| = $ _____	3. $|5\frac{3}{8}| = $ _____
4. $|36.25| = $ _____	5. $|-4\frac{7}{8}| = $ _____	6. $|-24.35| = $ _____
7. A bank account balance of −$45.00 = a debt of _____	8. A scuba diver at −22 feet = _____ feet below sea level.	9. A helicopter flying at 13,000 feet = _____ feet above sea level.

Activity Section 6: Comparing With and Without Absolute Value

Use number order or absolute value to answer the question.

1. Kamal has an account balance of −$12. Is his debt greater or less than $10?
2. Hector and Chloe are playing a video game. Hector has a score of −20. Chloe starts with 10 points but loses 29 points. Who has the higher score?

Activity Section 7: Ordered Pairs on a Coordinate Plane

Identify the quadrant of the location of each coordinate point.

1. (2, −2) Quadrant: _____	2. (6, 4) Quadrant: _____	3. (−5, −3) Quadrant: _____	4. (−1, −3) Quadrant: _____

Each pair of coordinate points are reflections of one another across the *x*- or *y*-axis.
Identify the axis.

5. (−7, −8) and (7, −8) Axis: _____	6. (−4, −1) and (−4, 1) Axis: _____

Standard: CCSS.Math.Content.6.NS.C.5, 6.NS.C.6a-c, 6.NS.C.7a-d, 6.NS.C.8

Plot and label each ordered pair on the coordinate plane.

7. A (−3, 6) Quadrant: _____

8. B (1, −3) Quadrant: _____

9. C (−4, 2) Quadrant: _____

10. D (−3, −3) Quadrant: _____

11. E (4, 4) Quadrant: _____

12. F (−2, −5) Quadrant: _____

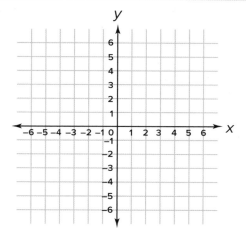

Activity Section 8: Graphing Integers and Rational Numbers

Plot each ordered pair on the coordinate plane.

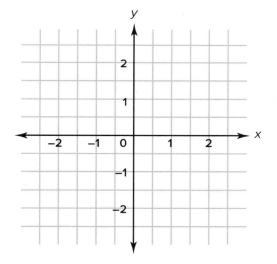

1. A (−2, 0)	2. B ($-1\frac{1}{2}$, $-\frac{1}{2}$)
3. C ($\frac{1}{2}$, −1.5)	4. D (1.5, −2)
5. E (−2, −2)	6. F (0, $\frac{1}{2}$)
7. G (1.5, $1\frac{1}{2}$)	8. H (−1, 0.5)

Activity Section 9: Graphing and Finding Distance on Coordinate Planes

Find the distance between the two coordinate points.

1. (8, −2) and (−2, −2)	2. (−4, −1) and (−4, 5)	3. (5, −2) and (5, −4)	4. (−4, −3) and (−1, −3)
Distance: _____	Distance: _____	Distance: _____	Distance: _____

5. Explain two different ways of finding the distance between two coordinate points:

☀ UNDERSTAND

Understand the meaning of what you have learned and apply your knowledge.

You will be asked to order rational numbers, both positive and negative.

Activity Section

The temperatures at Great Heights Ski Resort were recorded at four different times in one 24-hour period. The temperatures are listed in the table below.

Time	Temperature
9 PM	3.3°F
12 AM	−2.3°F
3 AM	−2.45°F
6 AM	−3.2°F

List the temperatures in order from warmest to coldest. Darian thinks it was coldest at 3 AM. Do you agree with him? Why or why not?

Standards: CCSS.Math.Content.6.NS.C.7b, CCSS.Math.Practice.MP1, MP2, MP3, MP4, MP6, MP7, MP8

DISCOVER

You've found the reflection of one point before. Use this knowledge to help you reflect an object over an axis on a coordinate plane. Reflections are used every day. Where else do you see reflections?

Activity Section

Leia plotted the rectangle on the coordinate plane below. Its points are listed in the table. Reflect the rectangle ABCD across the *x*-axis. Label the rectangle EFGH. List the ordered pairs of your new rectangle in the table. *Hint:* You know that when you reflect points, one coordinate stays the same and one turns into its opposite. Which coordinate stays the same when you reflect across the *x*-axis?

Ordered Pairs	
Point	**Reflection**
A (−5, −2)	E (_____ , _____)
B (−3, −2)	F (_____ , _____)
C (−3, −5)	G (_____ , _____)
D (−5, −5)	H (_____ , _____)

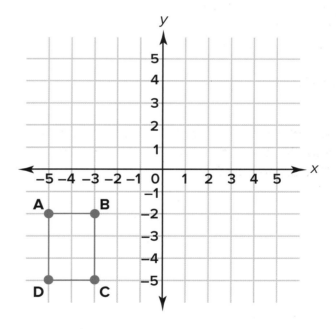

CORE Expression Concepts

Numerical Expressions with Exponents

UNPACK THE STANDARD
You will write and evaluate expressions with exponents.

LEARN IT: An *exponent* tells how many times a number will be multiplied. The number that is multiplied is called the *base.*

$$5 \times 5 \times 5 \times 5 = 5^4 \quad \leftarrow \text{exponent}$$
$$\text{base}$$

A *numerical expression* is a math phrase that doesn't have an equal sign. You can simplify expressions using the Order of Operations:

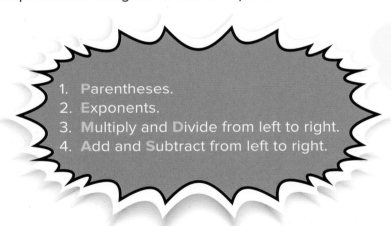

1. **P**arentheses.
2. **E**xponents.
3. **M**ultiply and **D**ivide from left to right.
4. **A**dd and **S**ubtract from left to right.

think! The phrase, "Please Excuse My Dear Aunt Sally," can help you remember the Order of Operations!

Example: Simplify $(2 \times 4) + 2^3 - 4 \div 2$.

Step 1:	Step 2:	Step 3:	Step 4:
Follow the operations inside parentheses.	Find the value of exponents.	Multiply and divide from left to right.	Add and subtract from left to right.
$(2 \times 4) + 2^3 - 4 \div 2$	$8 + 2^3 - 4 \div 2$	$8 + 8 - 4 \div 2$	$8 + 8 - 2$
$8 + 2^3 - 4 \div 2$	$8 + 8 - 4 \div 2$	$8 + 8 - 2$	$16 - 2$
			14

think!
$2 \times 2 \times 2 = 8$

Standard: CCSS.Math.Content.6.EE.A.1

PRACTICE: Now you try

Simplify each expression.

1. $(2 + 2)^2 \times 3 - 1$	2. $4^2 - (2 \times 4) + 3$	3. $8 \times 3^2 - 6 \times 3$	4. $100 \div (4 + 1)^2$
5. $(15 - 3)^2 \div 12$	6. $3^3 - (6 + 4) \div 5$	7. $56 \div (3 + 5) + 2^4$	8. $3 + (12 \times 6) \div 3^2$

Your friend was absent from school on the day your teacher explained numerical expressions with exponents. Explain to him or her how to find the value of this expression: $(2 \div 2) + 2 \times 2^2 - 2$. Show your work and write your explanation here.

ACE IT TIME!

	yes	no
Did you underline the question in the word problem?	○	○
Did you circle the numbers or number words?	○	○
Did you box the supporting details or information needed to solve the problem?	○	○
Did you draw a picture or a graphic organizer and write a math sentence to show your thinking?	○	○
Did you label your numbers and your picture?	○	○
Did you explain your thinking and use math vocabulary words in your explanation?	○	○

Math Vocabulary

add

base divide

exponent

multiply

order of operations

parentheses

subtract

MATH ON THE MOVE

Roll the dice! Roll a die 5 times. Write an expression with the numbers you roll. Try to include at least 3 different operations and one exponent in your expression. Use the Order of Operations to find the value!

Writing Expressions

UNPACK THE STANDARD
You will write expressions using variables.

LEARN IT: An *algebraic expression* is an expression that contains at least one variable. A *variable* is a letter that represents an unknown number. You can pick any letter you want to use as a variable.

Example: Jarred makes comic books. He charges $4 for each book he sells. Write an algebraic expression to show how much he earns.

Step 1:	Step 2:	Step 3:
Decide on the variable.

The variable is the unknown part. You don't know how many books Jarred sells.

Let's choose the variable *"b"* to represent the number of books he sells. | Decide which operation to use.

To find out how much he earned, you can add or multiply. Since you don't know how many times to add, you can show this using multiplication. | Write the expression.

$4 \times b$

think! What if you picked "x" as the variable? It would look like the multiplication symbol. Here are ways to show multiplication without the "x" symbol so you don't get them confused:

$4x$ $4(x)$ $4 \cdot x$ |

Pay close attention to what the problem is asking you to solve! This is how you decide which operation to use.

PRACTICE: Now you try

Write an algebraic expression for each of the following statements.

1. 32 subtracted from *y*	2. 45 divided by *m*
Hint: You can show division with either a ÷ symbol or a / symbol (like with fractions).
3. 102 more than *f*	4. *z* times as many as 18
5. 5 more than the quotient of 36 divided by *g*	6. 2 less than the product of 7 and *n*

Standard: CCSS.Math.Content.6.EE.A.2a

7. Braelyn is 3 years older than her brother. Her brother is *b* years old. How old is Braelyn?	**8.** Gregg has *a* apps in each of the 6 folders on his tablet. How many apps does he have in all?
9. Taylor buys *t* T-shirts at $9 each and *p* pairs of pants at $20 each. How much does she spend in all?	**10.** The Newton Middle School chorus has 5 fewer members than twice the number of students in the photography club. Let *p* represent the number of students in the photography club. How many students are in chorus?

Julius buys *n* graphic novels at $12 each and 3 bookmarks at $*b* each. He writes the expression $12n \times 3b$ to represent how much money he spends. Is Julius right? Why or why not? Show your work and explain your thinking on a piece of paper.

ACE IT TIME!

	yes	no
Did you underline the question in the word problem?	○	○
Did you circle the numbers or number words?	○	○
Did you box the supporting details or information needed to solve the problem?	○	○
Did you draw a picture or a graphic organizer and write a math sentence to show your thinking?	○	○
Did you label your numbers and your picture?	○	○
Did you explain your thinking and use math vocabulary words in your explanation?	○	○

Math Vocabulary

algebraic expression

operation

variable

MATH ON THE MOVE

Describe a situation that can be written using a variable. Ask a partner to write the algebraic expression that matches. Take turns describing different situations and writing matching expressions. Remember, an expression does not include an equal sign or an answer!

Identifying Parts of Expressions

UNPACK THE STANDARD
You will use mathematical terms to identify parts of an expression.

LEARN IT: Expressions can be described in two different parts: terms and coefficients. The **terms** of an expression are the parts that are separated by operations. A **coefficient** is the number that a variable is multiplied by.

Example: Identify the parts of the expression 6 times *m* plus 5.

Step 1:	Step 2:	Step 3:
Write the expression using math operations. 6*m* + 5	Identify the terms. $\boxed{6m} + \boxed{5}$ 6*m* and 5 are the terms because they are separated by an addition symbol.	Identify the coefficients. 6*m* + 5 The variable is multiplied by 6, so 6 is the coefficient.

think!
6*m* is the same as 6 x *m*. Why is it one term and not two? What are you adding to 5? The product of 6 and *m*. A **product** is one term.

You can also use words to describe numeric expressions.

Example: Write a word expression for 3 × (4 + 7).

Step 1:	Step 2:
Identify the terms of the expression. The first term is the number 3. The second term is what you multiply 3 by: the sum of 4 + 7. You can treat things in parentheses as one term, just like you can treat 6*m* as one term.	Identify the operations in the expression. Use words in place of the operations. 3 times the sum of 4 and 7

think!
Why is it not 3 times four plus 7? Remember your Order of Operations: Multiplying comes first! That would be 3 x 4 + 7. You say 3 times the **sum** because that shows you must find the sum before you can multiply. Using the word **sum** means you need parentheses.

Standard: CCSS.Math.Content.6.EE.A.2b

PRACTICE: Now you try

Identify the terms and coefficients of each expression.

| 1. $2x - (6 - 1)$

terms: _____ and _____

coefficient: _____ | 2. $(3 \times 4) + 8n$

terms: _____ and _____

coefficient: _____ |

Describe each expression with words.

3. $12 \times (45 \div 9)$	4. $4a - 2b$
5. $45 + (8 \times 5)$	6. $8 \times (9.5 - 3.6)$
7. $60 \div (5.5 + 4.5)$	8. $(2.1 \times 3.45) - 6.5$

Explain how the expression $3 \times (3 + 12)$ differs from $3 \times 3 + 12$. Write a word expression for both. Show your work and explain your thinking on a piece of paper.

ACE IT TIME!

Math Vocabulary

numerical expression

order of operations

parentheses

	yes	no
Did you underline the question in the word problem?	○	○
Did you circle the numbers or number words?	○	○
Did you box the supporting details or information needed to solve the problem?	○	○
Did you draw a picture or a graphic organizer and write a math sentence to show your thinking?	○	○
Did you label your numbers and your picture?	○	○
Did you explain your thinking and use math vocabulary words in your explanation?	○	○

MATH ON THE MOVE

Flip the cards! Using number cards 1–9, flip three cards. Create both a numerical and word expression with the three numbers. You can use the numbers in any order with any two operations. You can also use parentheses!

Evaluating Expressions

UNPACK THE STANDARD
You will evaluate expressions by substituting values for variables.

LEARN IT: Remember how you simplified numerical expressions to find their values? You can do the same with algebraic expressions if you know the value of the variables.

Example: Evaluate the expression $3(y + 3)^2$ for **y = 2**.

Step 1:	Step 2:	Step 3:	Step 4:
Substitute 2 for y. $3(y + 3)^2$ $3(2 + 3)^2$	Follow the Order of Operations. Simplify inside the parentheses first. $3(5)^2$	Simplify any exponents next. $3(5)^2$ $3(25)$ **think!** $5^2 = 5 \times 5 = 25$	Finish by multiplying. $3(25) = 75$

Remember that the expression will change value when the variable changes value.

PRACTICE: Now you try

Evaluate the following expressions.

1. $x^2 + 6$ for $x = 4$ $16 + 6 = 22$	**2.** $3d - 10$ for $d = 5$ $15 - 10 = 5$
3. $4g + 3 (10 + 2)$ for $g = 5$ $5 \quad (12)$ $20 + 36 = 56$	**4.** $3^3 - 27/n$ for $n = 3$ $27 - 9 = 18$
5. $25.5 - (10.2 + m)$ for $m = 1.4$ $25.5 - (10.2 + 1.4)$ 11.6	**6.** $12(3b \times 2)$ for $b = \frac{1}{2}$ 0.5

10.2
1.4
11.6

29.5
-11.6
13.9

I ♥ Algebra

$5x + 20 = 25$

Standard: CCSS.Math.Content.6.EE.A.2c

Evaluate the following expressions for $x = 2$ and $y = 3$.

7. $3x + 2y$	8. $15 - (2x - y)$	9. $(5y - 2) + x$
10. $12(x + y)$	11. $(20/x - 3y) + 15$	12. $(12y - 2.5) - (3x + 1.45)$

Tyrel and Henry were finding the volume of a cube. The cube has equal sides of s units. The volume of a cube is found by multiplying length times width times height. Tyrel says you could express this as s^3. Henry disagrees. Who is right? How do you know? What is the volume of the cube if $s = 3$? Show your work and explain your thinking on a piece of paper.

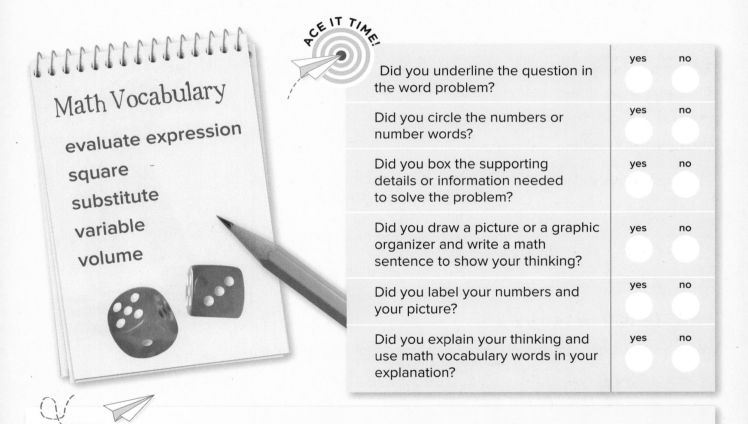

Math Vocabulary

evaluate expression

square

substitute

variable

volume

ACE IT TIME!

	yes	no
Did you underline the question in the word problem?	○	○
Did you circle the numbers or number words?	○	○
Did you box the supporting details or information needed to solve the problem?	○	○
Did you draw a picture or a graphic organizer and write a math sentence to show your thinking?	○	○
Did you label your numbers and your picture?	○	○
Did you explain your thinking and use math vocabulary words in your explanation?	○	○

MATH ON THE MOVE

Write an expression using any numbers and operations you choose. Use one variable in your expression. Roll a die; whatever you roll will be the value of the variable. Use the value to simplify your expression.

Generating Equivalent Expressions

UNPACK THE STANDARD
You will apply the properties of operations to write equivalent expressions.

LEARN IT: *Equivalent expressions* are equal to each other for any value of their variables. For example, $2 + x = x + 2$ because of the Commutative Property of Addition.

You can use many math properties to write equivalent expressions.

Example: Write an expression equivalent to $8(3 + z)$.

Step 1:	Step 2:
Use the Distributive Property.	Simplify.
$8(3 + z)$	$(8 \times 3) + (8 \times z)$
$(8 \times 3) + (8 \times z)$	$24 + 8z$

You can also write equivalent expressions by combining like terms.

Example: Write an expression equivalent to $y + y + y + y$.

Step 1:	Step 2:
Identify the variable.	Combine like terms.
The variable is y.	In this case, combine all of the y variables. Remember, multiplying is a quick way of doing repeated addition.
	$y + y + y + y = 4y$

PRACTICE: Now you try

Write an algebraic expression for each of the following statements.

1. $d + d + d + d + d$	2. $2x + 3y + 2x + 3y$	3. $6 + 3x + 7$
4. $3.5r + 1.5r$	5. $15g - 2h + 3g$	6. $2y + 2y + 2y$

Standard: CCSS.Math.Content.6.EE.A.3

Write equivalent expressions by using the Distributive Property.

7. $4(m + 12)$	8. $12(8 + p)$	9. $4s - 4t$
10. $6(a + 3b)$	11. $3.5(w + 2)$	12. $\frac{1}{2}(s + 10)$

Write two equivalent expressions you could use to show the perimeter of this square. Show your work and write your explanation here.

4s

ACE IT TIME!

	yes	no
Did you underline the question in the word problem?	○	○
Did you circle the numbers or number words?	○	○
Did you box the supporting details or information needed to solve the problem?	○	○
Did you draw a picture or a graphic organizer and write a math sentence to show your thinking?	○	○
Did you label your numbers and your picture?	○	○
Did you explain your thinking and use math vocabulary words in your explanation?	○	○

Math Vocabulary

equivalent expression

expression

perimeter

variable

MATH ON THE MOVE

Have a discussion about equivalent expressions. What does the word "equivalent" mean in other situations in math? Why does the Distributive Property help us find equivalent expressions?

Identifying Equivalent Expressions

UNPACK THE STANDARD
You will identify when two expressions are equivalent.

LEARN IT: Now that you know what equivalent expressions are, use what you know to decide if two expressions are equivalent or not. You'll need to use the properties of addition and multiplication (Commutative, Associative, and Distributive).

	Addition	Multiplication
Commutative Property	$2 + a = a + 2$	$2 \times a = a \times 2$
Associative Property	$2 + (3 + a) = (2 + 3) + a$	$2(3 \times a) = (2 \times 3)a$
Distributive Property	$2(a + b) = 2a + 2b$	

Example: Find an expression equivalent to $6a + 2a - 3$.

Step 1:	**Step 2:**
Use the Distributive Property to combine like terms.	Add within the parentheses.
$6a + 2a - 3$	$(6 + 2)a - 3$
$(6 + 2)a - 3$	$8a - 3$

Example: Use the Greatest Common Factor (GCF) to identify an expression equivalent to $4a + 12b$. $4(a + 3b)$

Step 1:	**Step 2:**	**Step 3:**	**Step 4:**
Find the GCF of the coefficients.	Write the first term as a product of the GCF and another factor.	Write the second term as the product of the GCF and another factor.	Use the Distributive Property.
The coefficients are 4 and 12.	$4a + 12b = 4 \times a + 12b$		$4(a + 3b)$
The GCF of 4 and 12 is 4.		$4a + 12b = 4 \times a + 4 \times 3b$	

PRACTICE: Now you try

Decide if the expressions are equivalent. Circle True or False.

1. $y + y = 2y$ True or False	**2.** $3c - 6d = 3(c - 2d)$ True or False
3. $x + x + 6y = 2(x + 6y)$ True or False	**4.** $5(6a + 4b) = 20b + 30a$ True or False

Standard: CCSS.Math.Content.6.EE.A.4

Find an equivalent expression.

5. $6(3 + x)$	**6.** $3(2c - d)$	**7.** $m + m + m + m + m$
8. $32s + 12t$	**9.** $p \times p$ *Hint:* How is this different from $p + p$?	**10.** $15k - 10j$

The Screamer roller coaster at Great Days Amusement Park has 8 cars in each train. Each car has 6 seats. Carolina writes the expression $8t \times 6$ to find the number of seats when there are t trains on the track. She thinks the expression $14t$ is an equivalent expression. Do you agree? Why or why not? Can you think of another equivalent expression? *Hint:* You can check your answer by using a value for the variable. If $t = 2$, does $8t \times 6 = 14t$? *What about if $t = 3$?* Show your work and explain your thinking on a piece of paper.

ACE IT TIME!

Math Vocabulary

Distributive Property

equivalent expressions

Greatest Common Factor (GCF)

variables

	yes	no
Did you underline the question in the word problem?	○	○
Did you circle the numbers or number words?	○	○
Did you box the supporting details or information needed to solve the problem?	○	○
Did you draw a picture or a graphic organizer and write a math sentence to show your thinking?	○	○
Did you label your numbers and your picture?	○	○
Did you explain your thinking and use math vocabulary words in your explanation?	○	○

MATH ON THE MOVE

Make up word problems for real-life situations. Write an expression to match your problem. Can you find any equivalent expressions? For example: You have 2 packs of gum, and each pack has g pieces of gum. How many pieces do you have if you give away 4? $2g - 4$?

More Work with Writing Expressions

UNPACK THE STANDARD
You will use expressions with variables to solve real-world problems.

LEARN IT: Use what you have learned about expressions and variables to solve real-world problems. In each problem there will be an unknown. Represent it with a variable.

Example: Vicki makes and sells picture frames on an online website. She sells them at $7.00 each. She also charges a $3.00 shipping fee for each order. What is the total cost for an order?

Step 1:	Step 2:	Step 3:
Identify the unknown. Use a variable to represent this number.	Write a word expression to match the problem.	Write the algebraic expression that matches.
You don't know the number of picture frames a customer will order. Use the variable n to show this.	*The total cost equals the cost of each frame **times** the number of frames **plus** the shipping charge.*	$7.00(n) + $3.00

think! The shipping cost is charged per order, not per picture frame, so you add instead of multiply.

Sometimes you will be given a value for the variable. Use it to solve the expression.

Example: Vicki sold 4 picture frames in one order. What was the total charge for the order?

Step 1:	Step 2:
Substitute the number for the variable.	Simplify using the Order of Operations.
$7n + 3$	$7(4) + 3$
$7(4) + 3$	$28 + 3$
	$31 for the order

PRACTICE: Now you try

Write an expression to match each situation.

1. A new recipe calls for twice as many cups of flour as your favorite recipe. It also calls for 1 cup of brown sugar. How many cups of ingredients do you need?

   a. _____

   b. If your favorite recipe calls for $1\frac{1}{2}$ cup of flour, how many cups of ingredients does the new recipe need? _____

Standard: CCSS.Math.Content.6.EE.B.6

2. A produce stand receives a shipment of tomatoes in crates of 36 each. Each crate contains 3 damaged tomatoes that cannot be sold. How many tomatoes can the produce stand sell?

a. _____

b. If the stand receives 6 crates, how many tomatoes can the produce stand sell?

_____

3. A cell phone company charges $25.00 for the first 200 texts and $0.10 for each additional text. If Aiden went over the 200 text limit last month, how much was he charged?

a. _____

b. If Aiden goes over by 12 texts this month, how much will he be charged?

_____

4. Josie goes shopping at the mall. She buys 2 pairs of shoes for $23 each and several pairs of shorts for $9 each. How much money did she spend?

a. _____

b. If Josie buys 4 pairs of shorts, how much money did she spend?

_____

Jim is 4 years more than twice Kendrick's age. If Kendrick is 12 years old, how old is Jim? Write an expression to solve. Show your work and explain your thinking on a piece of paper.

Math Vocabulary

expression

substitute

variable

ACE IT TIME!

	yes	no
Did you underline the question in the word problem?	◯	◯
Did you circle the numbers or number words?	◯	◯
Did you box the supporting details or information needed to solve the problem?	◯	◯
Did you draw a picture or a graphic organizer and write a math sentence to show your thinking?	◯	◯
Did you label your numbers and your picture?	◯	◯
Did you explain your thinking and use math vocabulary words in your explanation?	◯	◯

MATH ON THE MOVE

Go back and simplify any of the expressions in this lesson by substituting a number for the variable. How do the answers change if the variable changes? What stays the same?

REVIEW

Stop and think about what you have learned.

Congratulations! You've finished the lessons for this unit. This means you've learned about numerical and algebraic expressions. You are able to identify parts of an expression, as well as evaluate them, both with and without variables.

 Now it's time to prove your skills with expressions. Solve the problems below! Use all of the methods you have learned.

Activity Section 1: Numerical Expressions with Exponents

Simplify the following expressions.

1. $48 \div (2^3 - 2)$	2. $3^3 - (4 \times 3) + 2$
3. $(36 - 32)^2 \div 4$	4. $(4 + 2)^2 \times 2 - 4$
5. $(12 + 18) - 5^2 + (4 \times 2)$	6. $(3^3 - 2^2) - (2 \times 5) \div 5$
7. $72 \div (3 \times 12) + (2^4 - 4)$	8. $12 + (12 \times 12) - 12^2$

Activity Section 2: Writing Expressions

Write expressions to match each situation. Make sure to simplify each expression as much as possible.

1. 12 more than g	2. 18 less than x
3. y divided by 4	4. n times as many as 2
5. 4 less than the quotient of 42 and t	6. 3 more than the product of 12 and x
7. Candace has 12 more CDs than her younger brother Troy. Troy has n number of CDs. How many CDs does Candace have?	8. Olivia made 5 more than twice as many texts this month than she did last month. Last month she made t number of texts. How many texts did she make this month?
9. Erik uploaded 3 e-books to his e-reader at $6 each, and b e-books at $12 each. How much did he spend on e-books?	10. Annie makes 6 goody bags for her birthday party. She puts 3 stickers, 2 bracelets, and c lollipops in each bag. Write an expression to show how many treats she is sharing in all.

Standards: CCSS.Math.Content.6.EE.A.1, 6.EE.A.2a-c, 6.EE.A.3, 6.EE.A.4, 6.EE.B.6

Activity Section 3: Identifying Parts of Expressions

Identify the terms and coefficient of each expression. Fill in the blanks.

1. $(4 + 3) \times 4n$ terms: _____ and _____ coefficient: _____	**2.** $(12x + 2) - (5 \times 3)$ terms: _____ and _____ coefficient: _____

Describe each expression with words.

3. $3 \times (7 + 5)$	**4.** $4z - 3y$
5. $20 \div (2 \times 2)$	**6.** $(2b) + (3 \times 2)$

Activity Section 4: Evaluating Expressions

Solve the following problems.

1. $3^2 + x$, where $x = 6$	**2.** $\frac{14}{d}$, where $d = 2$
3. $36 - h(3 \times 2)$, where $h = 4$	**4.** $2^5 + x^3$ where $x = 3$
5. $4(y + 2)$, where $y = \frac{1}{4}$	**6.** $(2t \times 1.2) + 3.6$, where $t = 2.7$

Evaluate the following expressions, where $x = 3$ and $y = 5$.

7. $(4x + 3y) + 2$	**8.** $30 - (3x + 3y)$	**9.** $(7y + 2) + 2x$
10. $\frac{24}{2x} + (2 + y)$	**11.** $x^2(4 \times 2y)$	**12.** $(4.4 + 2.5x) + 1.2y$

Activity Section 5: Generating Equivalent Expressions

Fill in the blanks and answer the questions. Write equivalent expressions by combining like terms.

1. $f + f + f$	2. $5g + 12 + 3g$	3. $18 - 6 - 2v$
4. $45 + 7y + 3 + 2y$	5. $p \times p$	6. $3m + 2m + 3m + 3$

Write equivalent expressions by using the Distributive Property.

7. $6(k + 2)$	8. $(2 + v) \times 4$	9. $7.5(t + 3)$
10. $4(x + 2y)$	11. $\frac{1}{2}(r + 12)$	12. $g(8 + 4)$

Activity Section 6: Identifying Equivalent Expressions

Use the operation properties or GCF to find an equivalent expression.

1. $12(v + 6)$	2. $40m + 8m$	3. $2(8 - w)$
4. $40a - 24b$	5. $3(g + 6)$	6. $12j + 32k$

 Standards: CCSS.Math.Content.6.EE.A.1, 6.EE.A.2a-c, 6.EE.A.3, 6.EE.A.4, 6.EE.B.6

Activity Section 7: More Work with Writing Expressions

Solve the following problems. Write your expression in its simplest form.

1. An apartment complex has 6 buildings. Each building has 3 floors and *p* number of apartments on each floor. Write an expression to show how many apartments there are inside the apartment complex.

   a. _____

   b. If there are 4 apartments on each floor, how many apartments are there in all?

   _____

2. Stephan and his brother each have a tablet. They both have 4 music apps and *a* game apps on their tablet. Write an expression to show how many apps they have together.

   a. _____

   b. If they both have 6 game apps, how many apps do they have in all?

   _____

3. Zahara downloads 3 songs onto her laptop for $1.50 each and *s* songs for $2.00 each. Write an expression to show how much money she spends on song downloads.

   a. _____

   b. If Zahara downloads four $2.00 songs, how much does she spend in all?

   _____

4. Sophia is saving up to buy a new cell phone. She has $44 saved already, and saves $10 a week from her babysitting job. Write an expression to show how much money she will have in *n* weeks.

   a. _____

   b. How much money will Sophia have after 6 weeks?

   _____

UNDERSTAND

Understand the meaning of what you have learned and apply your knowledge.

Writing and evaluating expressions is a big part of algebraic thinking. Understanding variables and operations is the key to evaluating expressions.

Activity Section

Tasha has two bookshelves in her bedroom. One shelf is $4.6a + 3$ inches long. The other shelf is 4 times as long. Write an expression to show the length of the longer shelf. Use what you know about expressions to simplify and write an equivalent expression for the longer bookshelf.

Explain how you got your answer.

Standards: CCSS.Math.Content.6.EE.B.6, 6.EE.A.3, CCSS.Math.Practice.MP1, MP2, MP4, MP6, MP7, MP8

 DISCOVER

Discover how you can apply the information you have learned.

Variables and expressions are all around us! Once you learn to use variables and mathematical properties, it is easy to "plug in" a variable and solve.

Activity Section

The expression $1.8C + 32$ shows us how to convert from degrees Celsius to degrees Fahrenheit. The variable C represents the temperature in degrees Celsius. Last summer, Johanna and her family went on a trip to the Bahamas. The temperature there hit a high of 31° Celsius. Johanna said it was hotter in the Bahamas than back at home in Michigan, where the temperature was 86° Fahrenheit. Do you agree with her? Why or why not? *Hint:* Make sure both temperatures use the same unit so you can compare.

CORE
Equation Concepts

Solving Equations

UNPACK THE STANDARD
You will solve equations to find the value of their variables.

LEARN IT: An *equation* is a statement where two quantities are equal. Equations have two expressions joined by an equal sign. Like an expression, an equation can include variables.

To find the value of a variable in an equation, you have to answer the question: Which value of the variable makes this equation true?

Example: $24 + n = 36$

Step 1:	**Step 2:**
Solve the equation by using the inverse, or opposite, operation.	Substitute 12 for *n* to check your answer.
$$\begin{array}{r} 24 + n = 36 \\ -24 \qquad -24 \\ \hline n = 12 \end{array}$$ **think!** How can you get the variable alone? You can use subtraction to remove 24 from the expression on the left. Do the same to the right.	$$24 + n = 36$$ $$24 + 12 = 36$$ *The expressions are equal. You solved the equation!*

PRACTICE: Now you try

Solve the following equations.

1. $6 + x = 44$ Check the equation:	**2.** $y - 12 = 25$ Check the equation:
3. $7n = 42$ Check the equation:	**4.** $a \div 3 = 12$ Check the equation:
5. $975 = c + 635$ Check the equation:	**6.** $\frac{s}{6} = 112$ Check the equation:

think! This is a multiplication problem. What is the opposite of multiplication?

Standard: CCSS.Math.Content.6.EE.B.5

Mohammad is 64 inches tall. He is 16 inches taller than his younger sister, Mari. What is Mari's height? Write an equation and use inverse operations to solve. Show your work and write your explanation here.

Math Vocabulary

addition
equation
substitute
subtraction
variable

ACE IT TIME!

	yes	no
Did you underline the question in the word problem?	◯	◯
Did you circle the numbers or number words?	◯	◯
Did you box the supporting details or information needed to solve the problem?	◯	◯
Did you draw a picture or a graphic organizer and write a math sentence to show your thinking?	◯	◯
Did you label your numbers and your picture?	◯	◯
Did you explain your thinking and use math vocabulary words in your explanation?	◯	◯

MATH ON THE MOVE

Talk about it! Why do you apply the opposite of the given operation to both sides of an equation? Think about finding equivalent fractions—why do you do the same to the numerator and denominator?

Solving Equations in Real-World Contexts

UNPACK THE STANDARD
You will write and solve equations to solve real-world problems.

LEARN IT: Use what you know about writing expressions to write equations for real-world problems. You can solve for unknown variables just like you did in the last lesson.

Example: Brent spent $64 last year downloading music to his smartphone. The songs cost $2 each. How many songs did he download?

Step 1:	Step 2:
Write an equation to match the situation. $$2n = 64$$	Solve the equation. $2n = 64$ $2n \div 2 = 64 \div 2$ $n = 32$ **think!** Remember to solve using the inverse opertion!

PRACTICE: Now you try

think! You've solved problems like this without an equation before. If you want to solve using subtraction, can you write an equation using addition?

Write an equation with a variable for each situation. Solve.

1. Jillian has been taking dance lessons for 4 years longer than Kali. If Jillian has been taking dance lessons for 9 years, how long has Kali been taking dance lessons? Equation: _____ Solve:	2. Vito makes a goal to read 20 pages of his book each day. The book is 360 pages long. How many days will it take Vito to read the entire book if he sticks to his goal? Equation: _____ Solve:
3. The temperature in the morning was 17 degrees cooler than it was in the afternoon. If the afternoon temperature was 76 degrees, what was the morning temperature? Equation: _____ Solve:	4. Malik is helping his family build a fence around their vegetable garden. The garden is square and has a perimeter of 72 feet. What is the length of each side of the garden? Equation: _____ Solve:

Standard: CCSS.Math.Content.6.EE.B.7

5. Sari scored a 91 on her math test. This is 8 points higher than what she scored on her previous math test. What did Sari score on her previous math test?

Equation: _____

Solve:

6. A sporting goods store has 36 boxes of baseball cleats. Each box holds the same amount of cleats. There are 432 cleats in all. How many cleats are in each box?

Equation: _____

Solve:

Anthony is helping his parents make dinner. He follows a recipe for macaroni and cheese, which calls for $\frac{5}{8}$ cup of milk. After he pours the milk, there is $\frac{7}{8}$ cup of milk left in the carton. Write and solve an equation to find out how much milk was in the carton when Anthony started. Show your work and explain your thinking on a piece of paper.

ACE IT TIME!

	yes	no
Did you underline the question in the word problem?	○	○
Did you circle the numbers or number words?	○	○
Did you box the clue words that tell you what operation to use?	○	○
Did you use a picture to show your thinking?	○	○
Did you label your numbers and your picture?	○	○
Did you explain your thinking and use math vocabulary words in your explanation?	○	○

Math Vocabulary

equation
inverse operation
variable

MATH ON THE MOVE

Write equations to represent events in your daily life. Think about cooking, time, travel, and money. What other real-world events could use equations?

Writing Inequalities

UNPACK THE STANDARD
You will write inequalities using inequality symbols.

LEARN IT: An inequality is a mathematical sentence that compares two expressions that are not equal. It uses the inequality symbols >, <, ≥, and ≤. The symbols > and < mean "greater than" and "less than." The symbol ≥ means "greater than or equal to," and the symbol ≤ means "less than or equal to."

Example: Circle the TRUE inequalities and explain.

(3 > 1)	(10 + 5 ≥ 10)	(10 + 5 ≥ 15)	10 + 5 ≥ 20
3 is greater than 1.	15 is greater than or equal to 10.	15 is greater than or equal to 15.	NOT TRUE! 15 is NOT greater than or equal to 20.

You can write inequalities based on real-world situations by using a variable to show possible solutions.

Example: You need at least $2 to buy a bag of oranges at the fruit stand. How much money do you need?

Think about the words used to describe the situation! The words "at least" mean the answer could be equal to 2 or greater than 2.

Inequalities can have an infinite, or endless, number of solutions. You can show the possible solutions on a number line.

Example: $n < 3$	**Example:** $n \leq 3$
An open circle at the 3 means that 3 is NOT a possible solution.	A closed circle at the 3 means that 3 is a possible solution.
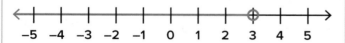	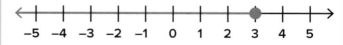
This number line does NOT include the number 3. It is described by the inequality $n < 3$, or "n is less than 3."	This number line includes the number 3. It is described by the inequality $n \leq 3$, or "n is less than or equal to 3."

PRACTICE: Now you try

Write an inequality for each situation.

1. Clarence has more than 4 tennis balls.	2. Zion runs no more than 5 miles each day.

3. Kobe can spend no more than $25 at the mall.	4. To ride the roller coaster, you must be at least 48 inches tall.

Write True or False to tell if the inequality is correct.

5. $100 - 56 < 45$	6. $13 \times 2 > 27$	7. $81 \div 9 \leq 9$

Write an inequality to match the number line.

8. 	9. 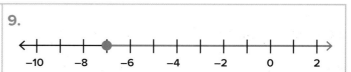

Chrystal has 3 times as many photos saved to her computer as she does songs. She has at least 20 songs. Write an inequality to show how many photos Chrystal has saved to her computer. Show your work and write your explanation here.

ACE IT TIME!

	yes	no
Did you underline the question in the word problem?	○	○
Did you circle the numbers or number words?	○	○
Did you box the supporting details or information needed to solve the problem?	○	○
Did you draw a picture or a graphic organizer and write a math sentence to show your thinking?	○	○
Did you label your numbers and your picture?	○	○
Did you explain your thinking and use math vocabulary words in your explanation?	○	○

Math Vocabulary

inequality

variable

MATH ON THE MOVE

Have a discussion. Explain the difference between $x < 5$ and $x \leq 5$. What do these inequalities represent?

Solving Inequalities

UNPACK THE STANDARD
You will solve inequalities by testing given values from a set of numbers.

LEARN IT: There may be many values that make an inequality true. This means there can be more than one solution to an inequality.

Example: All of Terrah's cousins are younger than 14 years old. You can describe this with the inequality $c < 14$. Determine if $c = 13$ and $c = 15$ are possible solutions.

Check:	**Check:**
Substitute the value $c = 13$ into the inequality.	Substitute the value $c = 15$ into the inequality.
$c < 14$	$c < 14$
$13 < 14$	$15 < 14$
TRUE!	FALSE!
$c = 13$ is a possible solution.	$c = 15$ is NOT a possible solution.

Any number that makes the inequality true can be included in a **solution set.**
For example, {13, 10, 7, 4} are just some of the ages that can be included in this solution set.
What are some others?

think!
What if Terrah had a cousin who was less than one year old? How would you write that number? What about a baby who is less than one month old? Remember, there are 12 months in a year.

PRACTICE: Now you try

Which values from the specified sets make the inequalities true?

1. $2x > 100$	2. $65 > 75 - m$
{40, 50, 60, 70} _____	{13, 12, 11, 10} _____
3. $\frac{1}{2}y \geq 5$	4. $\frac{60}{w} \leq 20$
{6, 8, 10, 12} _____	{2, 3, 4, 5} _____

Standard: CCSS.Math.Content.6.EE.B.5

Determine whether or not the given value of the variable is a possible solution. Write True or False.

5. $x > 4.5$; $x = 4.6$ _____	**6.** $n \leq -3$; $n = -2$ _____
7. $82 - g \geq 62$; $g = 21$ _____	**8.** $12/3 < z$; $z = 4.5$ _____

Jocelyn's class is having a discussion about voting. Their teacher tells them that you must be at least 18 years old to vote in the United States. That means Jocelyn and her classmates need to wait at least six more years until they can vote.

Does the inequality $a + 6 \geq 18$ describe the possible ages of students in Jocelyn's class? Which of the numbers in this solution set make the inequality true? {10, 11, 12, 13} How do you know? Show your work and explain your thinking on a piece of paper.

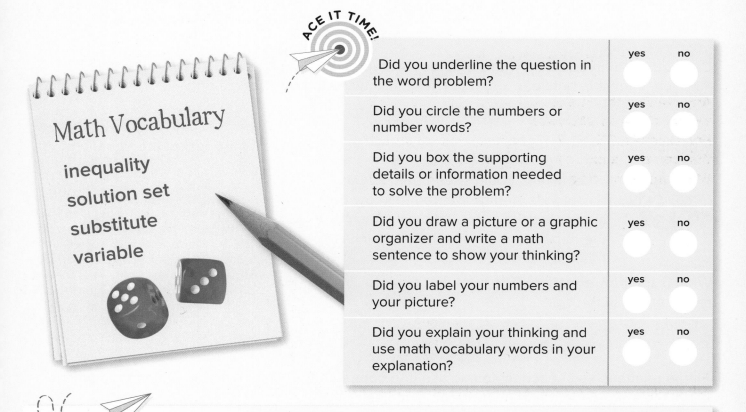

ACE IT TIME!

Math Vocabulary

inequality
solution set
substitute
variable

	yes	no
Did you underline the question in the word problem?	○	○
Did you circle the numbers or number words?	○	○
Did you box the supporting details or information needed to solve the problem?	○	○
Did you draw a picture or a graphic organizer and write a math sentence to show your thinking?	○	○
Did you label your numbers and your picture?	○	○
Did you explain your thinking and use math vocabulary words in your explanation?	○	○

MATH ON THE MOVE

Write an inequality using any numbers, one variable, and an inequality symbol of your choice. Roll a die. Substitute the number you rolled for your variable and determine if that inequality is true. If it's not, how can you change the inequality to make it true?

Independent and Dependent Variables

UNPACK THE STANDARD
You will analyze the relationship between independent and dependent variables.

LEARN IT: Did you know that you can solve equations with more than one variable? In some cases, there are two types of variables: *independent* and *dependent* variables. An independent variable can change freely. A dependent variable changes *depending* on the independent variable.

Example: Tyler was downloading songs for his smartphone. Below is a table that compares the cost of his downloads to the number of songs he bought.

Number of songs	x	1	2	3	4	5
Cost ($)	y	2	4	6	8	10

Which of the variables, x or y, is independent?
Which is dependent?

> **think!** What happens when you buy things? The number of songs determines the cost. Tyler can choose to buy a different number of songs. The cost depends on his choice. This means y is the dependent variable! The independent variable is x.

Can you write an equation with variables that represent this situation? Analyze the table. Find a relationship between x and y: The cost is twice the number of songs.

$$y = 2x$$

Write the dependent variable alone on one side. Its value is set by the rest of the equation.

What if Tyler could spend only $$d$ on downloads, and he wanted to know how many songs (s) he could buy? Which is the dependent variable now? Which is the independent variable?

What is the new equation? The number of songs represents half the cost.

$$s = \frac{d}{2}$$

> **think!** Now, the number of songs Tyler can buy is limited by the amount he can spend. Tyler can choose a different limit. The number of songs he can buy depends on that limit. This means s is the dependent variable now! The independent variable is d.

PRACTICE: Now you try

Find a relationship in each table and use it to complete the table. Write an equation to match. Label the independent and dependent variables.

1.

x	y
1	3
2	4
3	5
4	

2.

y	z
5	2
6	3
7	4
8	

Standard: CCSS.Math.Content.6.EE.C.9

Find a relationship in each table and use it to complete the table. Write an equation to match. Label the independent and dependent variables.

3.

Boxes of cereal (b)	Total Cost (c)
1	3.50
2	7.00
3	

Aimee is buying cereal, and she doesn't know how much it will cost to buy b boxes.

Independent variable: _____

Dependent variable: _____

Equation: _____

4.

Number of pizzas (p)	Total Cost (c)
1	16
2	32
3	

George is ordering pizza for a party, and he has a limit to how much he can spend.

Independent variable: _____

Dependent variable: _____

Equation: _____

Kayleigh loves to read. Each month for 5 months, she reads 3 books. Make a table to show the relationship between the number of months, m, and the number of books, b, she has read. Which is the independent variable? Which is the dependent variable? How do you know? Write an equation to represent the relationship. Show your work and explain your thinking on a piece of paper.

Math Vocabulary

dependent variable

equation

independent variable

variable

ACE IT TIME!

	yes	no
Did you underline the question in the word problem?	○	○
Did you circle the numbers or number words?	○	○
Did you box the supporting details or information needed to solve the problem?	○	○
Did you draw a picture or a graphic organizer and write a math sentence to show your thinking?	○	○
Did you label your numbers and your picture?	○	○
Did you explain your thinking and use math vocabulary words in your explanation?	○	○

MATH ON THE MOVE

Connect to science! Think of times you have discussed independent and dependent variables in science experiments at school. Do you see the connection?

Graphing Independent and Dependent Variables

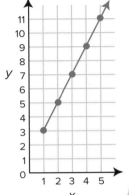

UNPACK THE STANDARD
You will graph independent and dependent variables.

LEARN IT: Remember what you know about graphing ordered pairs. In equations with two variables, you will have ordered pairs. As a rule, graph the independent variable on the x-axis. Graph the dependent variable on the y-axis.

Example: The table shows the relationship between x and y. If y changes depending on x, graph the ordered pairs. Write an equation to show the relationship.

See how the values of x, the independent variable, are on the x-axis. The dependent values are on the y-axis.

x	y
1	3
2	5
3	7
4	9
5	11

To find an equation, look at the table. If you don't see an immediate relationship, experiment. What happens if you multiply the x values by 2? By 3? By experimenting, you'll see that the y values are all one more than twice the x values.

$y = 2x + 1$

PRACTICE: Now you try

Graph the data and write an equation to match.

1. y = _____

x	1	2	3	4	5
y	3	6	9	12	15

y depends on x

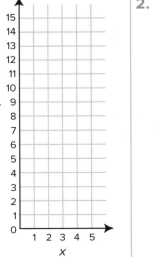

2. y = _____

x	1	2	3	4	5
y	1	3	5	7	9

x depends on y

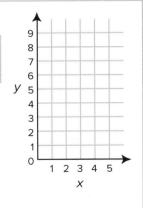

Standard: CCSS.Math.Content.6.EE.C.9

Keiser saves the same amount of money each year in his savings account. The table below shows the amount of money he has saved for the last five years. He wrote and graphed an equation to show the relationship between the amount of money saved (x) and the number of years (y). His work is shown below, but he made an error. Explain where Keiser went wrong.

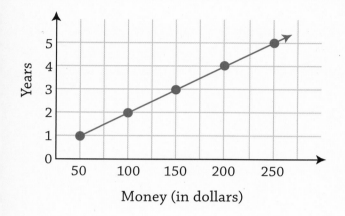

Years (y)	1	2	3	4	5
Money (x)	50	100	150	200	250

$x = 50y$

Math Vocabulary

dependent variable

independent variable

x-axis

y-axis

ACE IT TIME!

	yes	no
Did you underline the question in the word problem?	○	○
Did you circle the numbers or number words?	○	○
Did you box the supporting details or information needed to solve the problem?	○	○
Did you draw a picture or a graphic organizer and write a math sentence to show your thinking?	○	○
Did you label your numbers and your picture?	○	○
Did you explain your thinking and use math vocabulary words in your explanation?	○	○

MATH ON THE MOVE

Think about it! What are some strategies for identifying independent and dependent variables? How do you find the relationship between the two to write an equation? How do you know which is the x and which is the y variable?

REVIEW

Congratulations! You've finished the lessons for this unit. This means you have learned about solving equations and inequalities.

Now it's time to prove your skills with equation concepts. Solve the problems below! Use all of the methods you have learned.

Activity Section 1: Solving Equations

Find the value of the variable.

1. $13 + x = 64$	**2.** $9n = 810$
Check the equation:	Check the equation:
3. $a \div 7 = 7$	**4.** $z - 22 = 62$
Check the equation:	Check the equation:
5. $159 = y + 112$	**6.** $\dfrac{t}{4} = 128$
Check the equation:	Check the equation:

Standards: CCSS.Math.Content.6.EE.B.5, 6.EE.B.7, 6.EE.B.8, 6.EE.C.9

Activity Section 2: Solving Equations in Real-World Contexts

Solve the following problems.

1. Mrs. Hopkins baked enough cookies to give each of her children 6 cookies. If she baked 24 cookies, how many children does she have?

   Equation: _____

   Solve:

2. Keagan keeps her DVDs in a binder that holds 4 DVDs on each page. She has a total of 88 DVDs. How many pages in the binder are filled?

   Equation: _____

   Solve:

3. The high temperature in Los Angeles one day was 78 degrees. The next day, the high was 5 degrees warmer. What was the next day's high temperature?

   Equation: _____

   Solve:

4. Travis earns $12 for each lawn he mows in his neighborhood. He wants to earn $60 to buy a video game. How many lawns does Travis need to mow to reach his goal?

   Equation: _____

   Solve:

5. A shipment of skateboards comes in boxes of 14. Carl's Skate Shop received a shipment of 112 skateboards. How many boxes were in the shipment?

   Equation: _____

   Solve:

6. At the end of the month, Tyrell could do 120 sit-ups in one day. This was 3 times as many sit-ups as he was able to do at the beginning of the month. How many sit-ups was Tyrell able to do at the beginning of the month?

   Equation: _____

   Solve:

Activity Section 3: Writing Inequalities

Write an inequality to describe the situation.

1. Justin sends more than 2 text messages a day.	2. Adina uploads no more than 3 books a month.
3. Luis has a budget of spending no more than $15 a month on music.	4. All of Nora's siblings are at least 5 years old.

Determine whether the inequality is true. Write True or False.

5. $130 - 25 > 125$	6. $18 \times 6 > 109$	7. $\frac{120}{30} \leq 4$
8. $18 \geq 6 \times 4$	9. $56 < 3 + 8(7)$	10. $12 - 3 + 4 < 15$

Write an inequality for the graph. Use n for the variable.

11.	12.
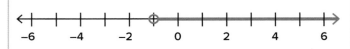	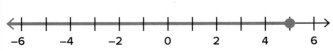

Activity Section 4: Solving Inequalities

Solve to find the values from the solution sets that make the inequalities true.

1. $50 > 80 - m$ $\{10, 20, 30, 40\}$ _____	2. $4x \geq 24$ $\{4, 5, 6, 7\}$ _____
3. $\frac{1}{4}m < 1$ $\{\frac{1}{4}, 1, 1\frac{1}{4}, 2\}$ _____	4. $\frac{360}{w} \leq 60$ $\{4, 6, 9, 12\}$ _____

Determine whether the given value of the variable is a possible solution to the inequality. Write True or False.

5. $x > 3.25$; $x = 3.24$ _____	6. $y \leq -12$; $y = -11$ _____
7. $16 - n \geq 12$; $n = 4$ _____	8. $\frac{24}{8} < z$; $z = 4$ _____
9. $m + 22 < 30$; $m = 9$ _____	10. $6c + 4 \geq 20$; $c = 3$ _____

Standards: CCSS.Math.Content.6.EE.B.5, 6.EE.B.7, 6.EE.B.8, 6.EE.C.9

Activity Section 5: Independent and Dependent Variables

Fill in the blanks and answer the questions.

1.

Months (m)	Number of books (b)
1	2
2	4
3	
4	

Equation: _____

Independent variable: _____

Dependent variable: _____

2.

Number of shoes (s)	Total cost (c)
1	12
2	24
3	
4	

Equation: _____

Independent variable: _____

Dependent variable: _____

3

x	y
1	5
2	6
3	7
4	

If x makes y change.

Equation: _____

Independent variable: _____

Dependent variable: _____

4

x	y
5	2.5
6	3
7	3.5
	4

If y makes x change.

Equation: _____

Independent variable: _____

Dependent variable: _____

Activity Section 6: Graphing Independent and Dependent Variables

Solve the following problems.

1. Shandi works at her family's frozen yogurt shop. The top selling item is the Fro-Yo's Supersize Sundae, which costs $6. Complete the table below to show the relationship between the sundae (s) and the total cost (c). Write an equation to match and graph it on the grid.

Number of Sundaes (s)	Total Cost (c)
1	
2	
3	
4	
5	

Ordered Pairs: _____

Equation: _____

Standards: CCSS.Math.Content.6.EE.B.5, 6.EE.B.7, 6.EE.B.8, 6.EE.C.9

UNDERSTAND

An input/output table is another way to represent variables. To find missing numbers in an input/output table, look for a pattern and write a rule based on the relationship between the variables. In an input/output table, the input is the independent variable, and the output is the dependent variable. You can then express the rule as an equation.

Activity Section

Find the missing outputs for this table. Find a rule for the table and write an equation.
Hint: Write a sentence describing the relationship between the input and the output values.

Input (x)	Output (y)
3	1
6	2
9	
12	
15	

Rule: _____ the input variable by _____

to get the output variable.

Equation: _____

DISCOVER

Discover how you can apply the information you have learned.

You solve equations in your daily life all the time, even if you don't realize it! Use your number sense and understanding of operations and variables to help you write and solve these equations.

Activity Section

Damon and Gabriel are on a baseball team. Their coach is ordering new jerseys for each player. The jerseys cost $22 each, and shipping is $8 for a whole order. To find out the total cost of the order, Damon suggests using the equation $t = 22j + 8j$. Gabriel suggests the equation $t = 22j + 8$. In both equations, t represents the total cost and j represents the number of jerseys. Who do you agree with and why?

Standards: CCSS.Math.Content.6.EE.B.7, CCSS.Math.Practice.MP1, MP2, MP3, MP4, MP6, MP7

Area of Triangles and Quadrilaterals

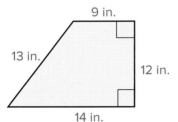

UNPACK THE STANDARD
You will use formulas find the area of triangles and quadrilaterals.

LEARN IT: Area is the measurement of how much space an object takes up on a surface. It is measured in square units (units²). Find the area of these shapes by using the formulas listed below. In these formulas, b is the base and h is the height.

triangles	parallelograms	trapezoids
think! The height is the distance from bottom to top. It is not the length of a slanted side of the triangle.		

triangles (8 cm, 6 cm)

$A = \frac{1}{2}bh$

$A = \frac{1}{2}(6 \times 8)$

$A = 24 \text{ cm}^2$

parallelograms (7 ft, 12 ft)

$A = bh$

$A = 12 \times 7$

$A = 84 \text{ ft}^2$

trapezoids (4 m, 5 m, 6 m)

$A = \frac{1}{2}(b_1 + b_2)h$

$A = \frac{1}{2}(4 + 6)5$

$A = 25 \text{ m}^2$

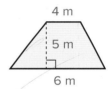

think!
Why is area in square units? You are multiplying feet × feet. Is that the same as feet²?

Example: Find the area of the quadrilateral.

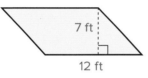

9 in.   13 in.   12 in.   14 in.

Step 1:	Step 2:
Identify the type of figure and the lengths you need.	Use the appropriate formula to find the area.
The figure is a trapezoid with bases 9 inches and 14 inches long. The vertical side is the height, 12 inches.	$A = \frac{1}{2}(9 + 14)12$ $A = \frac{1}{2}(23)12$ $A = 138 \text{ in.}^2$

PRACTICE: Now you try

Find the area of each polygon.

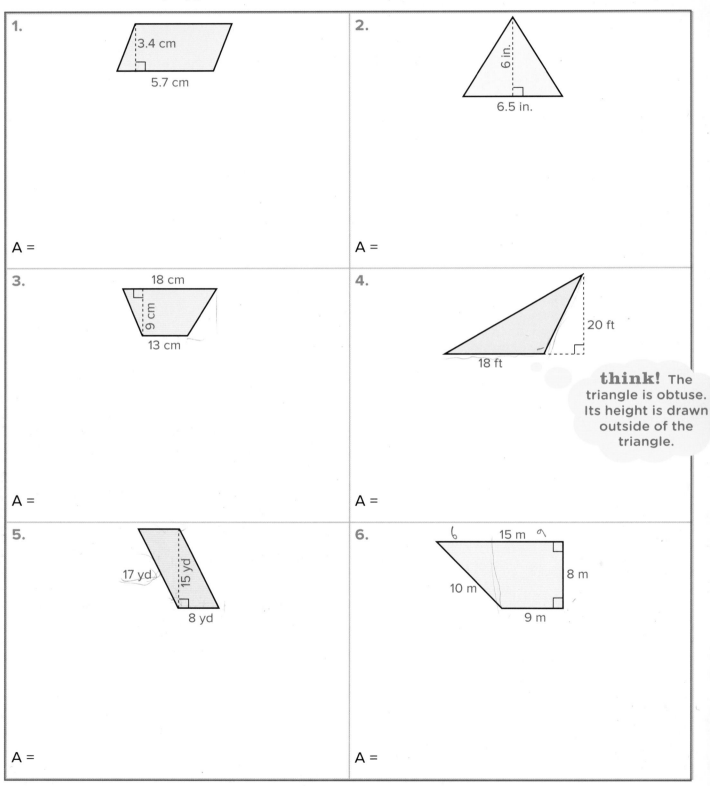

1. 3.4 cm, 5.7 cm

A =

2. 6 in., 6.5 in.

A =

3. 18 cm, 9 cm, 13 cm

A =

4. 20 ft, 18 ft

think! The triangle is obtuse. Its height is drawn outside of the triangle.

A =

5. 17 yd, 15 yd, 8 yd

A =

6. 15 m, 8 m, 10 m, 9 m

A =

A banner has four sides, one pair of which are parallel. The banner has one base that is 4 feet long, another base that is 8 feet long, and a height of 3.5 feet. What shape is the banner? What is the area of the banner? Explain how you know.

ACE IT TIME!

	yes	no
Did you underline the question in the word problem?	○	○
Did you circle the numbers or number words?	○	○
Did you box the supporting details or information needed to solve the problem?	○	○
Did you draw a picture or a graphic organizer and write a math sentence to show your thinking?	○	○
Did you label your numbers and your picture?	○	○
Did you explain your thinking and use math vocabulary words in your explanation?	○	○

Math Vocabulary

area

base

formula

parallelogram

quadrilateral

trapezoid

MATH ON THE MOVE

Have a discussion about how the area of a parallelogram is related to the area of a triangle when both figures have the same base and height.

Area of Composite Figures

UNPACK THE STANDARD
You will divide composite figures into familiar shapes in order to find areas.

LEARN IT: A *composite figure* is a larger figure that is made up of different, smaller shapes. The areas of those smaller shapes can then be found and added together to find the new area.

Example: Find the area of this regular hexagon by dividing it into familiar figures and adding those areas. Remember, a regular polygon has all sides the same length and all angles the same measure.

3.5 m
4 m

| **Step 1:** Draw line segments from the center of the hexagon to each vertex. *Hint:* You will end up with 6 triangles. 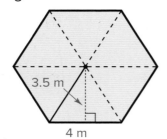 3.5 m 4 m | **Step 2:** Find the area of one of the triangles. $$A = \tfrac{1}{2}(4 \times 3.5)$$ $$A = 7 \text{ m}^2$$ The hexagon is regular, so each triangle has the same base length, 4 m. The heights are also the same, 3.5 m. | **Step 3:** Find the area of the hexagon. There are 6 triangles, each with the same area. Multiply the area of one triangle by 6. $$A = 6 \times 7 \text{ m}^2$$ $$A = 42 \text{ m}^2$$ |

PRACTICE: Now you try

Find the area of each composite figure.

| 1. 5 ft   5 ft 6 ft 5 ft **think!** You can divide this figure into a parallelogram and a triangle. A = | 2. 6 m   6 m 6 m 4 m 6 m 6 m A = |
| 3. 5 m 3 m 2 m   4 m A = | 4. 8 in. 10 in. 6 in. 8 in.   16 in. A = |

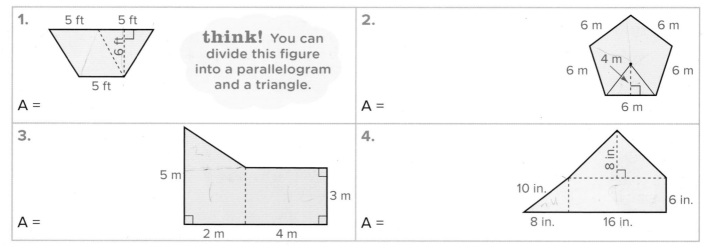

The figure shows the floor of a room. If wall-to-wall carpeting is installed, how many square feet of carpeting will be needed? Explain how you know. Show your work and write your explanation here.

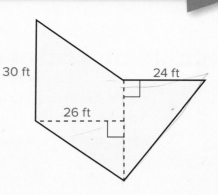

30 ft   24 ft

26 ft

Math Vocabulary

area
base
composite figure
parallelogram
quadrilateral
trapezoid

ACE IT TIME!

	yes	no
Did you underline the question in the word problem?	○	○
Did you circle the numbers or number words?	○	○
Did you box the supporting details or information needed to solve the problem?	○	○
Did you draw a picture or a graphic organizer and write a math sentence to show your thinking?	○	○
Did you label your numbers and your picture?	○	○
Did you explain your thinking and use math vocabulary words in your explanation?	○	○

MATH ON THE MOVE

Find objects in real life that are composite shapes, such as floors or gardens. Figure out how you can divide those figures into familiar shapes. Use a tape measure to find dimensions and estimate the areas.

Volume of Rectangular Prisms

UNPACK THE STANDARD
You will find the volume of rectangular prisms.

LEARN IT: Do you remember what volume is? **Volume** is the amount of space something takes up. It is different than area because area measures the space of a flat object (on a surface). Objects with area have two dimensions: base (b) and height (h). Objects with volume have three dimensions: length (l), width (w), and height (h). Volume is measured in cubic units (units^3).

Example: A jewelry box measures $5\frac{1}{2}$ units long, 2 units wide, and 3 units high. What is the volume of the box?

Use the formula
$V = l \times w \times h$ to solve.

$V = 5\frac{1}{2}$ units × 2 units × 3 units

$= \frac{11}{2} \times 2 \times 3$

$= \frac{66}{2}$

$= 33$ units^3

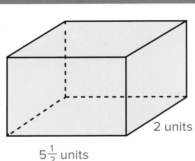

3 units

2 units

$5\frac{1}{2}$ units

think!
You can also solve by using the formula $V = Bh$, where B represents the area of the base. Remember, the base is flat! Can you say that the formula $A = bh$ could be written as $A = lw$? Why or why not?

PRACTICE: Now you try

Find the volume.

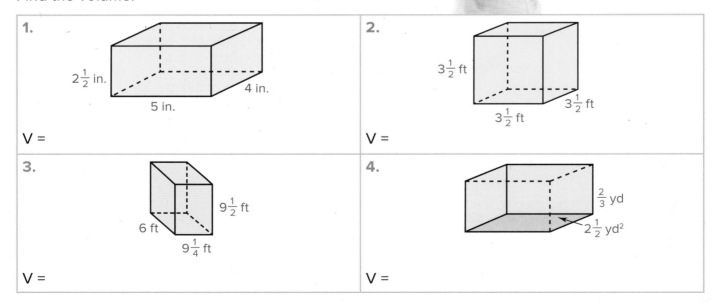

1.

$2\frac{1}{2}$ in.

4 in.

5 in.

V =

2.

$3\frac{1}{2}$ ft

$3\frac{1}{2}$ ft

$3\frac{1}{2}$ ft

V =

3.

$9\frac{1}{2}$ ft

6 ft

$9\frac{1}{4}$ ft

V =

4.

$\frac{2}{3}$ yd

$2\frac{1}{2}$ yd^2

V =

Standard: CCSS.Math.Content.6.G.A.2

5. A cereal box measures $7\frac{3}{4}$ inches long, 2 inches wide, and 12 inches high. What is the volume of the box?

6. A laundry basket is 2 feet long, $1\frac{1}{2}$ feet wide, and $1\frac{3}{4}$ feet high. What is the volume of the basket?

Chloe wants to fill a cooler with ice. The cooler is in the shape of a cube. One side of the cooler is $1\frac{1}{2}$ feet long. How many cubic feet of ice will it take to fill the cooler? Show your work and write your explanation here.

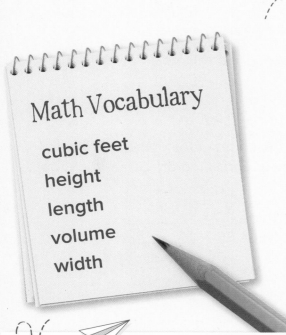

ACE IT TIME!

	yes	no
Did you underline the question in the word problem?	○	○
Did you circle the numbers or number words?	○	○
Did you box the supporting details or information needed to solve the problem?	○	○
Did you draw a picture or a graphic organizer and write a math sentence to show your thinking?	○	○
Did you label your numbers and your picture?	○	○
Did you explain your thinking and use math vocabulary words in your explanation?	○	○

Math Vocabulary

cubic feet

height

length

volume

width

MATH ON THE MOVE

Roll the dice! Roll four numbers. Use two of the numbers to make a fractional length. The other two numbers will be the width and the height. Find the volume of a rectangular prism with these measurements.

Polygons on the Coordinate Plane

UNPACK THE STANDARD
You will draw polygons on a coordinate plane.

LEARN IT: You have learned how to plot points on a coordinate plane. These can form the vertices of a polygon. **Vertices** are the points where two sides of a polygon meet.

Example: Three vertices of parallelogram ABCD are A (2, −2), B (−4, −2), and C (−2, 3). Find the coordinates of vertex D and graph the parallelogram.

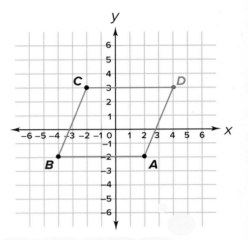

| **Step 1:** |
| Graph the coordinates *A, B,* and *C* on the coordinate plane. |
| **Step 2:** |
| Connect the points to form part of a parallelogram. |
| **Step 3:** |
| Find point *D* to complete the parallelogram. (4, 3) |

think! What are the properties of a parallelogram? You can count or use absolute value to find that side *BA* is 6 units long. Its parallel side, *CD*, should be the same length. Find the *x*-coordinate of *D* by putting *D* 6 units from *C*. The *y*-coordinate stays the same. This puts *CD* on a straight line, just like *BA*.

PRACTICE: Now you try

Solve the following problems.

1. Find the coordinates of *J* in rectangle *JKLM* and graph the point.

   Point *J* = (_____ , _____)
   Length of side *KL* = _____
   Length of side *ML* = _____

   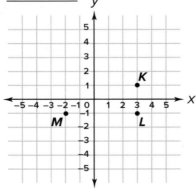

2. Find the coordinates of the unknown vertex of parallelogram *CDEF* and graph.

   Point *F* = (_____ , _____)
   Length of side *CD* = _____
   Length of side *FE* = _____

   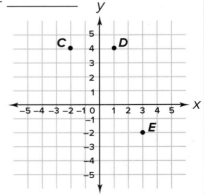

Standard: CCSS.Math.Content.6.G.A.3

3. Plot the points and connect to form a polygon.

D (−2, 2), E (3, 2), F (5, −2), G (−4, −2).

Name the polygon: _____

Length of side DE = _____

Length of side GF = _____

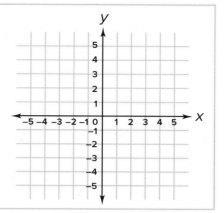

Peyton draws a polygon on a coordinate plane. Polygon *PQRST* has vertices with coordinates P (−4, 0), Q (−2, 3), R (2, 3), S (4, 0), and T (0, −3). What kind of polygon did she plot? How do you know? Plot the points and graph the polygon on the coordinate plane. Show your work and write your explanation here.

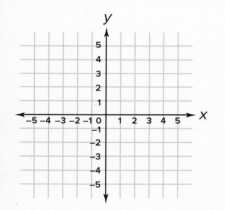

ACE IT TIME!

	yes	no
Did you underline the question in the word problem?	○	○
Did you circle the numbers or number words?	○	○
Did you box the supporting details or information needed to solve the problem?	○	○
Did you draw a picture or a graphic organizer and write a math sentence to show your thinking?	○	○
Did you label your numbers and your picture?	○	○
Did you explain your thinking and use math vocabulary words in your explanation?	○	○

Math Vocabulary

coordinate plane

polygon

vertices

MATH ON THE MOVE

Have a discussion. How does finding the length of a side of a polygon relate to finding the distance between two points on a coordinate grid?

Representing Three-Dimensional Figures Using Nets

UNPACK THE STANDARD
You will represent three-dimensional figures with nets.

LEARN IT: A figure with volume can also be called a three-dimensional figure because it has three dimensions: length, width, and height. These types of figures are identified by the shapes of their bases, the number of their bases, and the shapes of their faces.

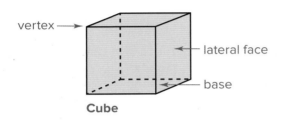

Cube

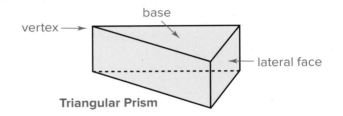

Triangular Prism

See how a cube has a square base and square sides. A triangular prism has a triangular base and rectangular sides. Both of these figures can be made using a net. A **net** is a two-dimensional, flat pattern that folds up to form a three-dimensional figure.

Example: What three-dimensional figure does the net below represent?

think!
Look at the base and sides in the figures above. There are more sides than bases. Since there are more triangles than squares, the triangles must be sides.

Step 1:
Identify the shapes that make up the net. This net is made from 4 triangles and one square. The square is the base, and the triangles are the faces.

Step 2:
Create and identify the figure. Think of folding the faces up around the base to form the three-dimensional figure. This is a pyramid. Since this has a square base, you can call it a square pyramid.

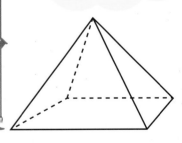

PRACTICE: Now you try

Identify the three-dimensional figure each net represents.

1.	2.	3.

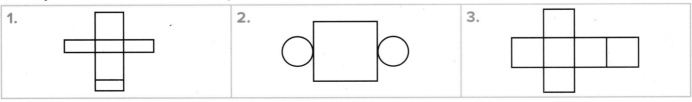

Standard: CCSS.Math.Content.6.G.A.4

4. A tent is shaped like the three-dimensional figure shown. What is the name of this figure? Draw a net to represent it.

Out of the 11 nets shown, Kylie thinks only 8 of them can be formed to make a cube. Do you agree with her? Why or why not? Circle all of the nets that can be used to form a cube. *Hint:* You can draw the nets on paper and try folding them up to see which will make a cube.

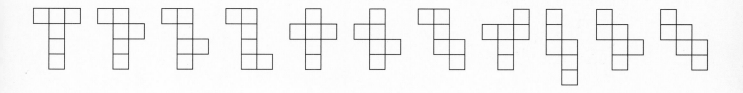

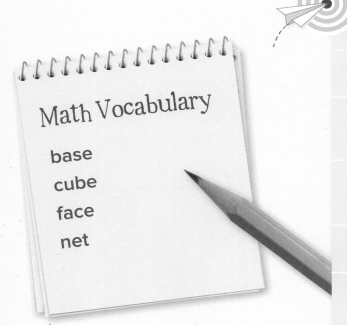

ACE IT TIME!

	yes	no
Did you underline the question in the word problem?	○	○
Did you circle the numbers or number words?	○	○
Did you box the supporting details or information needed to solve the problem?	○	○
Did you draw a picture or a graphic organizer and write a math sentence to show your thinking?	○	○
Did you label your numbers and your picture?	○	○
Did you explain your thinking and use math vocabulary words in your explanation?	○	○

Math Vocabulary

base

cube

face

net

MATH ON THE MOVE

Make your own net! Carefully cut open an empty box and unfold it to create a net. Be careful to only cut around certain edges and not across the faces! Cereal boxes work great, but look for other cardboard boxes you can use, like tissue boxes.

Using Nets to Find Surface Area

UNPACK THE STANDARD
You will use nets to find the surface area of three-dimensional figures.

LEARN IT: Remember that area measures the space taken up by a flat surface. A three-dimensional figure has many flat surfaces. This means that 3D figures have surface area. Surface area is the sum of the areas of all the bases and faces. Remember this clue: Sur*face area* is the **area** of the **faces**! That is why it is measured in square units.

Example: Use a net to find the surface area of the rectangular prism shown.

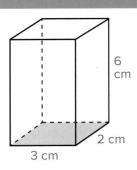

Step 1:	**Step 2:**
Draw a net of the figure. Label each face.	Find the area of each face using the formula $A = l \times w$. *Hint:* Look for congruent shapes!

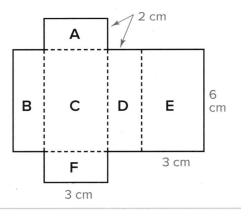

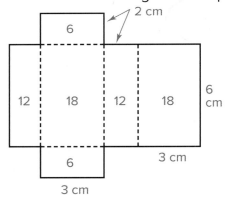

Step 3:

The surface area is the sum of the individual areas. 6 + 6 + 12 + 12 + 18 + 18 = **72 cm²**

PRACTICE: Now you try

Use a net to find the surface area of each solid figure.

1.

2.

Standard: CCSS.Math.Content.6.G.A.4

3. Arman is wrapping a gift that is shaped like the rectangular prism shown here. What is the least amount of wrapping paper he will need to cover the box?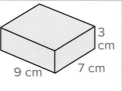

3 cm

9 cm   7 cm

4. Heather is painting a box with the dimensions shown here. What is the surface area of the box?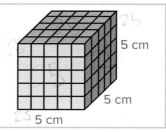

5 cm

5 cm

5 cm

The net of a square pyramid is shown below. Find the surface area of the solid figure. Explain how you found your answer. *Hint:* You learned the formula for the area of a triangle earlier in this unit. Show your work and write your explanation here.

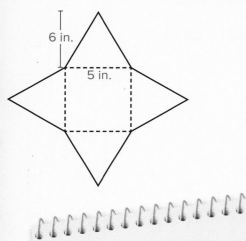

6 in.

5 in.

Math Vocabulary

area

net

square pyramid

surface area

triangle

ACE IT TIME!

	yes	no
Did you underline the question in the word problem?	◯	◯
Did you circle the numbers or number words?	◯	◯
Did you box the supporting details or information needed to solve the problem?	◯	◯
Did you draw a picture or a graphic organizer and write a math sentence to show your thinking?	◯	◯
Did you label your numbers and your picture?	◯	◯
Did you explain your thinking and use math vocabulary words in your explanation?	◯	◯

MATH ON THE MOVE

Use number cards #1–9. Flip three cards. Use the numbers to create a three-dimensional figure with these dimensions. Draw the net for this figure and find its surface area.

REVIEW

Stop and think about what you have learned.

Congratulations! You've finished the lessons for this unit. This means you've learned how to find the area of quadrilaterals and triangles. You know how to find the volume of rectangular prisms and how to find the surface area of a three-dimensional figure. You can also plot polygons on a coordinate plane.

Now it's time to prove your skills with geometry. Solve the problems below! Use all of the methods you have learned.

Activity Section 1: Area of Triangles and Quadrilaterals

Use the following formulas to find the area of each polygon.

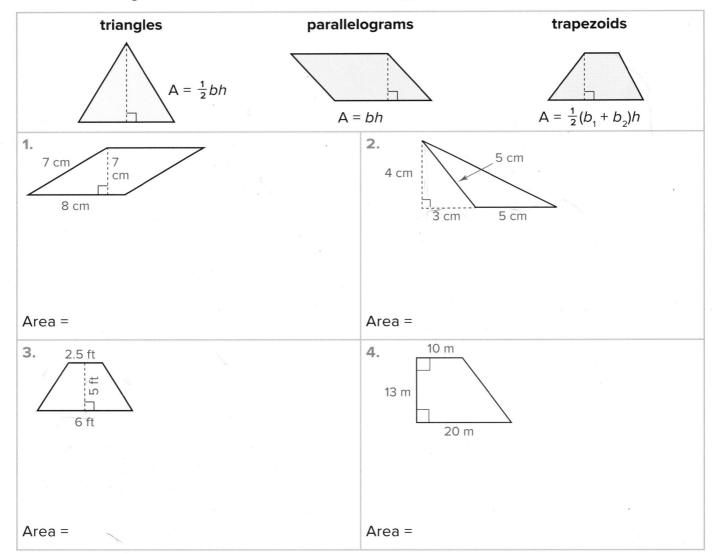

triangles	parallelograms	trapezoids
$A = \frac{1}{2}bh$	$A = bh$	$A = \frac{1}{2}(b_1 + b_2)h$

1.

7 cm   7 cm

8 cm

Area =

2.

4 cm   5 cm

3 cm   5 cm

Area =

3.

2.5 ft

5 ft

6 ft

Area =

4.

10 m

13 m

20 m

Area =

Standards: CCSS.Math.Content.6.G.A.1, 6.G.A.2, 6.G.A.3, 6.G.A.4

Activity Section 2: Area of Composite Figures

Solve the following problems.

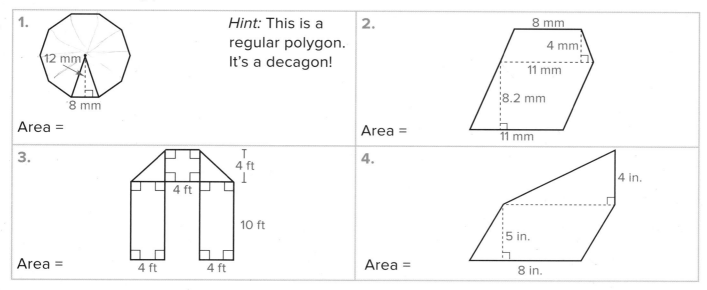

1.

12 mm

8 mm

Hint: This is a regular polygon. It's a decagon!

Area =

2.

8 mm

4 mm

11 mm

8.2 mm

11 mm

Area =

3.

4 ft

4 ft

10 ft

4 ft   4 ft

Area =

4.

4 in.

5 in.

8 in.

Area =

Activity Section 3: Volume of Rectangular Prisms

Solve the following problems.

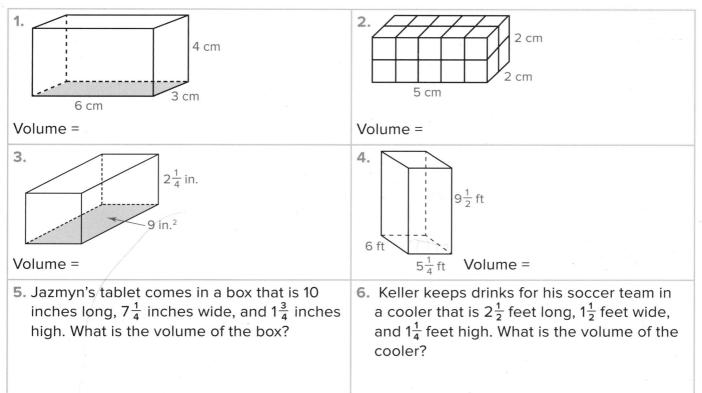

1.

4 cm

3 cm

6 cm

Volume =

2.

2 cm

2 cm

5 cm

Volume =

3.

$2\frac{1}{4}$ in.

9 in.²

Volume =

4.

$9\frac{1}{2}$ ft

6 ft

$5\frac{1}{4}$ ft   Volume =

5. Jazmyn's tablet comes in a box that is 10 inches long, $7\frac{1}{4}$ inches wide, and $1\frac{3}{4}$ inches high. What is the volume of the box?

6. Keller keeps drinks for his soccer team in a cooler that is $2\frac{1}{2}$ feet long, $1\frac{1}{2}$ feet wide, and $1\frac{1}{4}$ feet high. What is the volume of the cooler?

Activity Section 4: Polygons on the Coordinate Plane

Solve the following problem.

1. Plot the points on the coordinate plane and connect to form a polygon:

   D (−1, 2), E (3, 2), F (3, −3), G (−4, −3)   Name the polygon: _____

   Explain how you know: _____

   _____

   Length of side DE = _____   Length of side GF = _____

   Explain how you found the length of each side: _____

   _____

   _____

   _____

   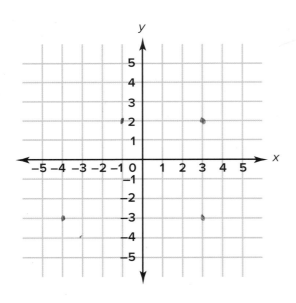

Standards: CCSS.Math.Content.6.G.A.1, 6.G.A.2, 6.G.A.3, 6.G.A.4

Activity Section 5: Representing Three-Dimensional Figures Using Nets

Identify the three-dimensional figure each net represents.

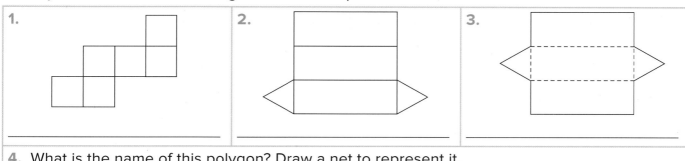

1. _____

2. _____

3. _____

4. What is the name of this polygon? Draw a net to represent it.

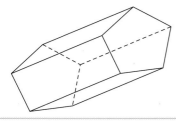

Activity Section 6: Using Nets to Find Surface Area

Use a net to find the surface area of each figure.

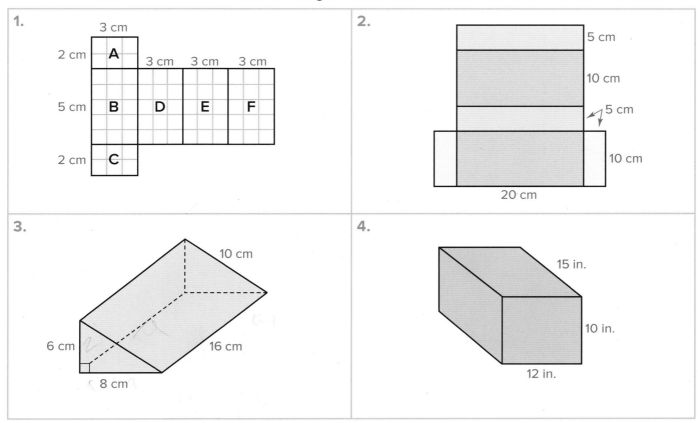

1.
3 cm
2 cm A
3 cm 3 cm 3 cm
5 cm B D E F
2 cm C

2.
5 cm
10 cm
5 cm
10 cm
20 cm

3.
10 cm
6 cm
16 cm
8 cm

4.
15 in.
10 in.
12 in.

UNDERSTAND

Understand the meaning of what you have learned and apply your knowledge.

Use what you know about finding the area of parallelograms and triangles to solve the problem below.

Activity Section

Find the area of the shaded region. Explain the steps you used to solve.

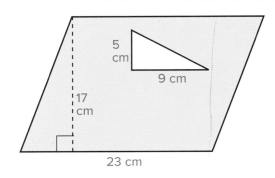

Standards: CCSS.Math.Content.6.G.A.1, CCSS.Math.Practice.MP1, MP2, MP4, MP6, MP7, MP8

Discover how you can apply the information you have learned.

Covering boxes with wrapping paper is a real-world example of surface area. Use what you know about surface area to solve the problem below.

Activity Section

Darnell found an interesting box he would like to reuse as part of his Earth Day recycling project. He wants to cover the box in green wrapping paper. What is the least amount of paper he will need to cover the entire box?

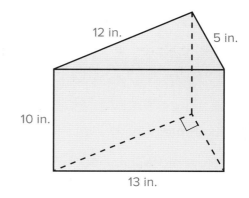

CORE Statistical Variability Concepts

Recognizing Statistical Questions

UNPACK THE STANDARD
You will recognize statistical questions.

LEARN IT: A *statistical question* asks about a set of data that can vary, or change. A statistical question has multiple answers rather than one single answer.

Example: Which of the following is a statistical question?

"How old will my classmates be on the last day of school this year?"

OR

"How old will I be on the last day of school this year?"

"How old will my classmates be on the last day of school this year?" IS a statistical question because the answers will vary. Different students will be different ages!

You will be only ONE age on that specific day. There is only one answer to "How old will I be on the last day of school this year?" Therefore this is NOT a statistical question.

think!
Which question has multiple answers? Which question only allows for one piece of data to be the answer?

PRACTICE: Now you try

Decide which of the questions are statistical and which are not. Write *statistical* or *not statistical* next to each question and explain why.

1. How tall are the boys in your class?
2. How tall is your classmate Ethan?
3. How many inches of rain did the state of Florida receive in June, 2014?

Standard: CCSS.Math.Content.6.SP.A.1

4. How many inches of rain does the state of Florida receive in June each year?

5. How long did it take you to get to school this morning?

6. How long did it take you to get to school each morning this week?

Tucker wants to collect data on how much time he and his classmates spend watching TV each week. He writes the question "How much time do you spend watching TV each week?" Is this a statistical question? Why or why not? Show your work and explain your thinking on a piece of paper.

ACE IT TIME!

	yes	no
Did you underline the question in the word problem?	◯	◯
Did you circle the numbers or number words?	◯	◯
Did you box the supporting details or information needed to solve the problem?	◯	◯
Did you draw a picture or a graphic organizer and write a math sentence to show your thinking?	◯	◯
Did you label your numbers and your picture?	◯	◯
Did you explain your thinking and use math vocabulary words in your explanation?	◯	◯

Math Vocabulary

data
statistical question
vary

MATH ON THE MOVE

Think about it. Why do you use statistical questions when gathering data? Why shouldn't you use questions that have only one answer? *Hint:* What about when asking questions about people? Are all people the same?

Measures of Center

UNPACK THE STANDARD
You will describe a set of data using measurements of center: median and mean.

LEARN IT: A *measure of center* is a single value used to describe the center, or middle, of a data set. To find the center of a data set, you need to find the mean or the median.

The **mean** is the average of the data set. To find an average, find the sum of the data points and divide by the total number of data points. The **median** is the middle value when the data set is listed in order from least to greatest.

Example: Find the mean and median of the data set: 12, 18, 13, 15, 16, 13

Step 1:	Step 2:
Find the mean. **think!** What is the sum of the data points? How many data points are there? The sum is: 12 + 18 + 13 + 15 + 16 + 13 = 87 Since there are 6 data points, the average is: 87 ÷ 6 = 14.5	List the data in order from least to greatest: 12, 13, 13, 15, 16, 18 Circle the number(s) in the middle of the list. In this example, there are two numbers in the middle. The median is the mean of the two numbers. 12, 13, (13, 15,) 16, 18 13 + 15 = 28 28 ÷ 2 = 14

The **mode** of the data is the data value, or values, that occur most often. Can you find the mode in the example above? Right! The mode is 13.

PRACTICE: Now you try

Find the mean, median, and mode of each data set.

1. Data set: 6, 9, 6, 8, 6

Mean: _____

Median: _____

Mode: _____

2. Data set: 26, 32, 26, 36, 32, 28

Mean: _____

Median: _____

Mode: _____
Hint: There can be more than one mode!

Standard: CCSS.Math.Content.6.SP.A.2, SPA.3, SP.B.5c

3. Data set: 201, 202, 205, 197, 205

   Mean: _____

   Median: _____

   Mode: _____

4. Data set: 1,203, 1,204, 1,202, 1,203

   Mean: _____

   Median: _____

   Mode: _____

Treyvon kept track of his scores for his latest math quizzes: 85, 90, 87, 93, 89, and 90. What is the mean of his scores? The median? The mode? Explain the steps you need to take to solve. Show your work and write your explanation here.

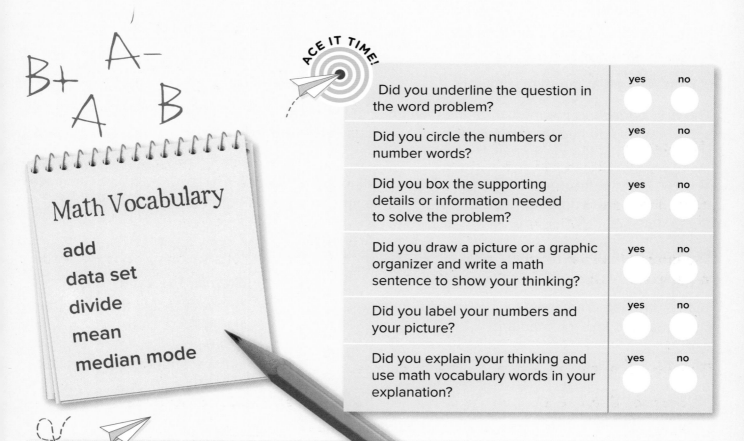

Math Vocabulary

add

data set

divide

mean

median mode

ACE IT TIME!

	yes	no
Did you underline the question in the word problem?	○	○
Did you circle the numbers or number words?	○	○
Did you box the supporting details or information needed to solve the problem?	○	○
Did you draw a picture or a graphic organizer and write a math sentence to show your thinking?	○	○
Did you label your numbers and your picture?	○	○
Did you explain your thinking and use math vocabulary words in your explanation?	○	○

MATH ON THE MOVE

Flip the cards! Using cards with digits #1–9, flip over six cards. Use these numbers to create a data set. Find the mean, median, and mode of this data.

Measures of Variation

UNPACK THE STANDARD
You will calculate the range of a set of data.

LEARN IT: Think about statistical questions. They can have many answers, and these answers can be different. Another way of saying this is that answers can vary. You can measure how they vary using *measures of variation.*

One measurement is *range*. The range is the difference between the lowest and highest data points. It shows how widely the data are spread.

Another measurement is interquartile range (IQR). To find IQR, you must split the data into fourths called quartiles. Count: $0, \frac{1}{4}, \frac{1}{2}, \frac{3}{4}, 1$. There are 5 numbers from 0 to 1. That means there are 5 measurements when you split into quartiles:

(0): the lowest data point (minimum)

$(\frac{1}{4})$: the first quartile

$(\frac{1}{2})$: the median of the whole data set

$(\frac{3}{4})$: the third quartile

(1): the highest number (maximum)

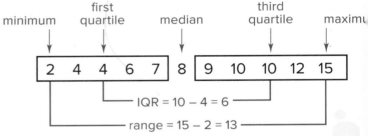

The **first quartile** is the median of the lower half of the data. You find it the same way as you find the median of the whole data set. The **third quartile** is the median of the upper half.

You can find the **interquartile range** (IQR) by finding the difference between the first and third quartiles. It shows the spread of the middle half of the data set.

think! There is an odd number of numbers in the set, so the median (8) is not included in either half.

Example: Find the range and IQR of the data set: 12, 16, 20, 13, 30, 18, 16, 10

Step 1:	**Step 2:**	**Step 3:**
Order the data from least to greatest and find the median.	Find the quartiles.	Subtract to find the range and the IQR.
10 12 13 16 ‖ 16 18 20 30	Lower half of the data: 10, <u>12</u>, <u>13</u>, 16 $\frac{12 + 13}{2} = 12.5$	Subtract the extremes to find the range. $30 - 10 = 20$
median = 16 $\frac{16 + 16}{2} = 16$	Upper half of the data: 16, <u>18</u>, <u>20</u>, 30 $\frac{18 + 20}{2} = 19$	Subtract the quartiles to find the IQR. $19 - 12.5 = 6.5$

think! There is an even number of numbers in the set, so the two middle numbers (16 and 16) are included in the halves.

PRACTICE: Now you try

Calculate the range and IQR.

1. 4, 5, 7, 9, 10, 12, 13	2. 5, 6, 6, 10, 10, 12, 16, 17	3. 4, 2, 3, 1, 5, 1, 8
range = _____	range = _____	range = _____
IQR = _____	IQR = _____	IQR = _____
4. 26, 1, 89, 31, 42, 15	5. 0.5, 9, 0, 10.5, 0.5, 6, 7, 5.5, 10	6. 900, 250, 645, 100, 150, 50, 225, 705
range = _____	range = _____	range = _____
IQR = _____	IQR = _____	IQR = _____

The ages of the volunteers at a hospital are: 16, 18, 19, 22, 58, 18, 17, 16, 25, 20, 16. Calculate the range and IQR. Explain how you got your answer. Show your work and explain your thinking on a piece of paper.

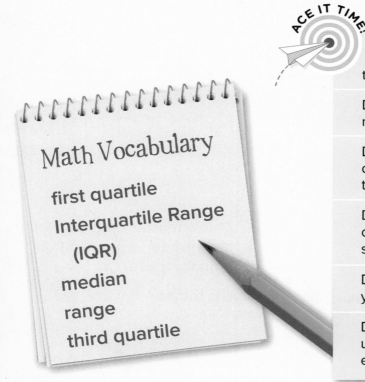

ACE IT TIME!

	yes	no
Did you underline the question in the word problem?	○	○
Did you circle the numbers or number words?	○	○
Did you box the supporting details or information needed to solve the problem?	○	○
Did you draw a picture or a graphic organizer and write a math sentence to show your thinking?	○	○
Did you label your numbers and your picture?	○	○
Did you explain your thinking and use math vocabulary words in your explanation?	○	○

Math Vocabulary

first quartile
Interquartile Range (IQR)
median
range
third quartile

MATH ON THE MOVE

Find the height in inches of 7 or more friends or family members. Calculate the range and IQR of your data.

Mean Absolute Deviation

UNPACK THE STANDARD
You will calculate the mean absolute deviation of a data set.

LEARN IT: The word "deviate" means to turn away from something. You can deviate from the route your GPS tells you to take. You can also measure how much your data deviates from the mean. This measure is the **mean absolute deviation** (MAD), and it shows the average distance data points are from the mean.

What do you remember about finding distance? How do you find the *difference* between one point and another?

Example: Five of your friends buy treats at a café. They spend the following amounts, in dollars: 2, 3, 4, 4, 5, 6. Find the MAD and use it to describe the data.

Step 1:	Step 2:	Step 3:
Find the mean of the data.	Find the distance of each data point from the mean.	Find the mean (average) of these deviations.
think! To find the distance from the mean, first you need to know the mean!	**think!** Distances can't be negative. How do you make sure you get a positive answer? Use absolute value!	**think!** The deviations 2, 1, 0, 0, 1, and 2 are a new data set. Find the mean like you normally would.
$\frac{2+3+4+4+5+6}{6} = 4$	$\|2-4\|=2$ $\|3-4\|=1$ $\|4-4\|=0$ $\|4-4\|=0$ $\|5-4\|=1$ $\|6-4\|=2$	$\frac{2+1+0+0+1+2}{6} = 1$ On average, the amount each friend spent varies by \$1.00 from the mean.

If the MAD is small, the data are very close to each other. This means they are similar. If the MAD is large, the data are spread out. This means they vary a lot.

PRACTICE: Now you try

Calculate the mean and MAD for each set. For real-world data sets, explain what the MAD represents.

1. 2, 3, 4, 2, 9
   mean = _____
   MAD = _____

2. 10, 60, 10, 30, 40
   mean = _____
   MAD = _____

3. 100, 250, 300, 250, 100, 650, 150, 200
   mean = _____
   MAD = _____

 Standard: CCSS.Math.Content.6.SP.A.2, 6.SP.A.3, 6.SP.B.5c

4. 0.5, 2.5, 5, 7, 4.5, 8, 9.5, 8, 2, 6

mean = _____

MAD = _____

5. Speed limits (in miles per hour) on signs on the way to the park: 25, 50, 55, 45, 30, 5

mean = _____

MAD = _____

explanation = _____

6. Ages (in years) of sixth grade teachers at Manny's school: 26, 32, 35, 48, 62, 22, 45, 50

mean = _____

MAD = _____

explanation = _____

The table shows the heights of the five starting players on a girls' basketball team and the five girls chosen to compete on a gymnastics team. Find the mean and MAD for both data sets. Compare the two data sets. Show your work and explain your thinking on a piece of paper.

| Basketball Players' Heights (in.) | 65 | 70 | 72 | 68 | 70 |
| Gymnasts' Heights (in.) | 60 | 59 | 61 | 63 | 62 |

ACE IT TIME!

	yes	no
Did you underline the question in the word problem?	○	○
Did you circle the numbers or number words?	○	○
Did you box the supporting details or information needed to solve the problem?	○	○
Did you draw a picture or a graphic organizer and write a math sentence to show your thinking?	○	○
Did you label your numbers and your picture?	○	○
Did you explain your thinking and use math vocabulary words in your explanation?	○	○

Math Vocabulary

average

mean

Mean Absolute Deviation (MAD)

variable

MATH ON THE MOVE

Roll the dice! Roll a die 10 times. Find the mean and the MAD of those 10 values. Write a sentence explaining how much the data vary from the mean. Do you think the data can vary much? Why or why not? *Hint:* There are only 6 numbers on a die.

Dot Plots

UNPACK THE STANDARD
You will use a dot plot to describe data.

LEARN IT: You've learned how to measure ways that data vary. You can also describe data visually. A **dot plot** is a number line that shows the frequency of data. **Frequency** is the number of times something happens.

Example: The table shows the lengths, in centimeters, of infants born at a hospital on Sunday.

Lengths of infants (centimeters)				
47	50	51	49	50
52	45	48	60	53
49	50	56	50	51
51	50	51	48	52

Step 1:

Draw a number line. Choose a scale that allows you to show all the data.

The least value in the table is 45 centimeters.

The greatest value is 60 centimeters.

Many values differ by 1 centimeter.

A scale of 45 to 60, with intervals of 1, is a good choice.

Step 2:

Draw a dot to represent each point.

The length 47 centimeters appears once in the table.

Draw one dot above 47.

The length 50 centimeters appears five times in the table.

Draw five dots above 50.

Continue until all 20 data points are plotted.

think! Compare the dot plot to the table. Which makes it easier to see the center and spread of the data?

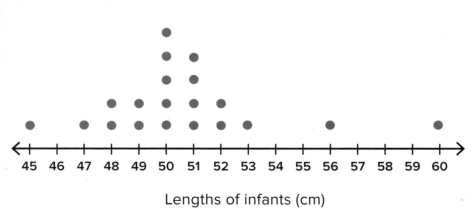

Lengths of infants (cm)

Standard: CCSS.Math.Content.6.SP.A.2, SP.B.4, SP.B.5a, SP.B.5b, SP.B.5c

Example: Jarrod is training to run a half marathon. He keeps track of how many miles he runs each day.

Look at the dot plot to answer these questions. They describe the data.

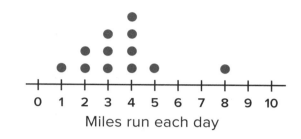

Miles run each day

What is the range?	*What is the median?*	*Are there any clusters in the data?*	*Are there any outliers?*	*Is the data symmetrical?*
Remember what you have learned!	The median is the average of the 6th and 7th numbers.	There are the most points at 3 and 4. This means that most days, Jarrod ran 3 or 4 miles.	Outliers are very different from the rest of the data.	Symmetry means the left and right sides of the plot look similar.
$8 - 1 = 7$	$$\frac{3 + 4}{2} = 3.5$$		The outlier is 8 miles. It is much greater than the other values.	This data is not symmetrical.
The range is 7 miles.	The median is 3.5 miles.			

think! What measurement can a cluster represent? What is the name for the data point that appears the most?

PRACTICE: Now you try

Use the dot plot to answer the questions about the data

The dot plot shows the number of texts Lauryn sends each day.

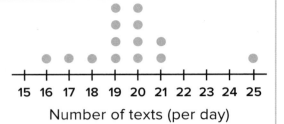

Number of texts (per day)

1. What does each dot represent?

2. What is the range?

3. What is the median number of texts?

4. What is the mode?

5. Describe any patterns in the data.

6. Are there any outliers?

Create and describe a dot plot.

The table shows the weights, in pounds, of boxes to be shipped.

7. Create a dot plot of these data. Be sure to label and number the number line.

Weights (lb)				
18	15	18	20	16
17	19	19	9	19
18	18	17	12	19
14	7	15	19	17

8. Describe the shape of the data.

Standard: CCSS.Math.Content.6.SP.A.2, SP.B.4, SP.B.5a, SP.B.5b, SP.B.5c

Create a dot plot based on the data shown here. Think of a situation these data could represent. Add a title to the frequency table. Write 5 statements of your own to describe the data set. Show your work and write your answer here.

5	4	6	7
4	6	5	7
7	5	10	3

ACE IT TIME!

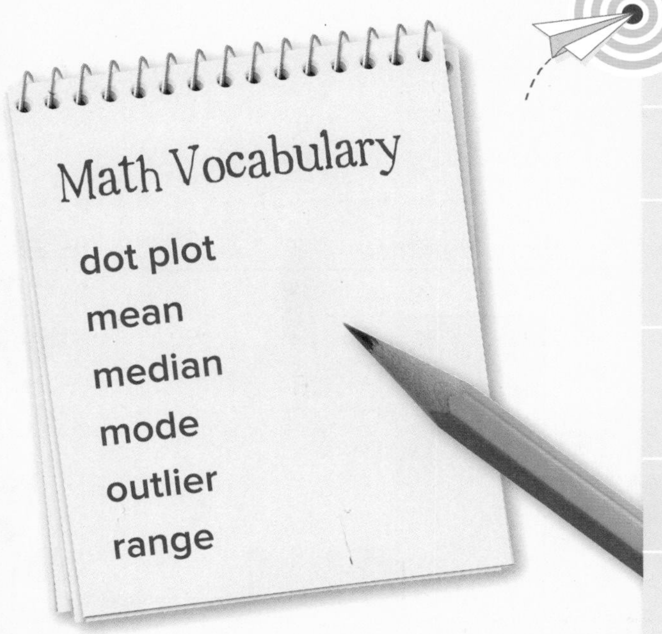

Math Vocabulary

dot plot
mean
median
mode
outlier
range

	yes	no
Did you underline the question in the word problem?		
Did you circle the numbers or number words?		
Did you box the supporting details or information needed to solve the problem?		
Did you draw a picture or a graphic organizer and write a math sentence to show your thinking?		
Did you label your numbers and your picture?		
Did you explain your thinking and use math vocabulary words in your explanation?		

MATH ON THE MOVE

Think of situations in your life where you can collect your own data. Collect the data and display it with a dot plot. Describe your data.

Histograms

UNPACK THE STANDARD
You will use histograms to show and describe sets of data.

LEARN IT: A *histogram* uses bars to show the frequency of data. Remember, frequency is how often something happens. To make a histogram from data, first group the data into equal *intervals*.

The table shows the heights of plants in a greenhouse.

Example: Create a histogram of these data.

Plant Heights (cm)					
2	4	4	5	5	7
8	9	10	11	12	13
13	13	14	18	19	22

Step 1:

Choose equal intervals. Think of intervals sort of like skip counting.

If you choose 0–4 cm as the first interval, the next interval has to start at 5.

Each interval must be the same size. So, the next interval is 5–9 cm.

The highest value in the table is 22, so choose intervals that will include values up to 22 cm.

Step 2:

Use a tally chart to count the number of data points that fall into each interval.

Interval	Tallies	Frequency
0–4	III	3
5–9	HHH	5
10–14	HHH II	7
15–19	II	2
20–24	I	1

Step 3:

Create the histogram.

List the intervals on the horizontal axis and frequencies on the vertical axis.

Draw a bar for each interval with no space between the bars.

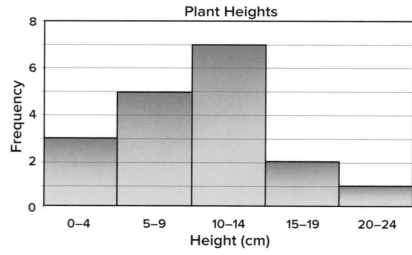

Standard: CCSS.Math.Content.6.SP.A.2, SP.B.4, SP.B.5a, SP.B.5c

Histograms can be used to describe data. Like dot plots, they give a sense of where the center and spread of a data set lies. Specifically, they show (1) shape, (2) the total number of data points, and (3) the interval with the greatest frequency.

Example: This histogram shows the scores earned by bowlers during a tournament. Each person bowled only one game.

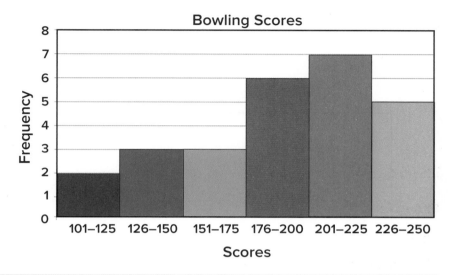

1. *What is the shape of the data?*

The bars are highest on the right. That means more of the data occurs to the right. Most scores were 176 or higher.

2. *How many bowlers participated in the tournament?*

Add the frequencies for the bars:

2 + 3 + 3 + 6 + 7 + 5 = 26

So, 26 bowlers participated.

3. *Which interval describes the most data points?*

The tallest bar has the highest frequency. The interval 201–225 has the most data points. So, more bowlers had scores of 201 to 225 than scores in any other interval.

PRACTICE: Now you try

Use histograms to show and describe data.

This list shows the number of runs a baseball team scored during 21 games last season: 0, 2, 3, 4, 4, 4, 5, 5, 6, 6, 6, 6, 7, 7, 7, 8, 8, 8, 8, 9, 9.

1. On the grid below, make a histogram of the data.

think! Choose equal intervals for the horizontal axis.

2. Describe the shape of the histogram.

3. Which interval has the greatest number of homeruns?

The histogram shows the weights, in pounds, of cats who are treated by a veterinarian.

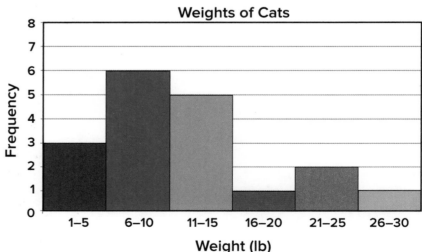

Weights of Cats

4. How many cats are treated by the veterinarian?

5. Describe the shape of the histogram.

Standard: CCSS.Math.Content.6.SP.A.2, SP.B.4, SP.B.5a, SP.B.5c

The table shows the ages of contestants on a game show. Make a histogram of the data in the space below. Does the interval with the most values show the mode? Explain. *Hint:* Can you find the frequency of each data point in the intervals? Explain your thinking.

Age (yrs)	17–20	21–24	25–28	29–32	33–36
Frequency	3	7	5	1	2

ACE IT TIME!

	yes	no
Did you underline the question in the word problem?		
Did you circle the numbers or number words?		
Did you box the supporting details or information needed to solve the problem?		
Did you draw a picture or a graphic organizer and write a math sentence to show your thinking?		
Did you label your numbers and your picture?		
Did you explain your thinking and use math vocabulary words in your explanation?		

Math Vocabulary

cluster
frequency table
histogram
interval

MATH ON THE MOVE

Roll two dice 10 times and record the sum of each roll. Make a histogram of the data. Describe the shape of the data.

Box Plots

UNPACK THE STANDARD
You will represent and describe data with box plots.

LEARN IT: A box plot shows the center and the spread of a set of data.

Example: The scores earned by eleven students on a math test are:
60, 70, 75, 75, 80, 80, 85, 90, 90, 95, and 100. Create a box plot to represent the data.

Step 1: Find the minimum and maximum of the data set. Then find the median and quartiles.	minimum · first quartile · median · third quartile · maximum 60 70 **75** 75 80 **80** 85 **90** 90 95 **100**
Step 2: Draw a number line. Plot points above the extremes, quartiles, and median. Draw a box from the first quartile to the third quartile. Divide the box at the median. Then draw a "whisker" from each extreme to the box.	minimum · first quartile · median · third quartile · maximum 60 65 70 75 80 85 90 95 100

The box shows the middle 50% of the data. So, about half of the students had scores from 75 to 90. The "whiskers" show the lower 25% and upper 25% of the data. So, about one-quarter of students had scores of 75 or below and about one-quarter had scores of 90 or higher.

Standard: CCSS.Math.Content. 6.SP.A.2, 6.SP.B.4, 6.SP.B.5b, 6.SP.B.5c

You can use box plots to describe the center and spread of data.

Example: The box plot represents the monthly costs of rentals in the town of Marsville. Use the box plot to describe the center and spread of the data.

Rents in Marsville ($)

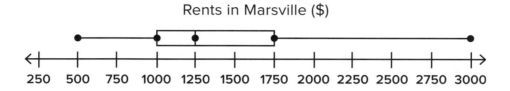

Step 1:	**Step 2:**	**Step 3:**
What is the median? *Hint:* The box is divided at the median. The median cost of a rental in Marsville is $1,250 per month. The median rental cost, $1,250, shows the center of the data.	What is the range? *Hint:* Subtract the values at the ends of the whiskers. range = 3,000 − 500 = $2,500 The range shows the spread of all the data. Rental costs in Marsville range from $500 to $3,000 per month. The range is great—a $2,500 difference between the least expensive and the most expensive.	What is the interquartile range (IQR)? *Hint:* Subtract the values at the ends of the box. IQR = 1,750 − 1,000 = $750 The IQR shows the spread of the middle 50% of the data. Half of the rentals in Marsville cost $1,000 to $1,750 per month. The IQR is much less than the range, only $750.

PRACTICE: Now you try

Use a box plot to represent and describe the data.

The ages, in years, of used cars on a car lot are: 1, 2, 2, 3, 4, 5, 6, 6, 8, 9, 12

1. Use the number line to make a box plot of the data.

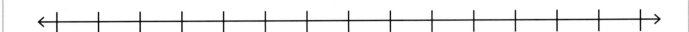

2. Identify each measure on the box plot: extremes: _____ and _____

median: _____   first and third quartiles: _____ and _____

3. Find the range. Show your work.

4. Find the interquartile range. Show your work.

The box plot represents the number of points Arnob scored per game last basketball season.

Points Arnob Scored Per Game

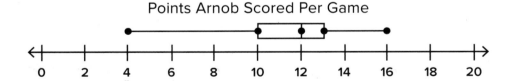

5. What is the median number of points Arnob scored per game?

6. In what percentage of the games did Arnob score 10 or fewer points?

7. In what percentage of the games did Arnob score 10 to 13 points?

The box plot shows the high temperatures for each day last summer in Miltown. Identify the extremes, median, and quartiles. Use the range and interquartile range to describe the spread of the data. Show your work and write your explanation here.

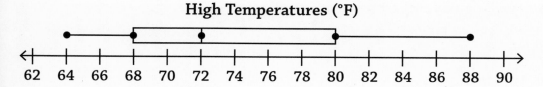

High Temperatures (°F)

Math Vocabulary

box plot

extreme

Interquartile Range (IQR)

median

range

ACE IT TIME!

	yes	no
Did you underline the question in the word problem?		
Did you circle the numbers or number words?		
Did you box the supporting details or information needed to solve the problem?		
Did you draw a picture or a graphic organizer and write a math sentence to show your thinking?		
Did you label your numbers and your picture?		
Did you explain your thinking and use math vocabulary words in your explanation?		

MATH ON THE MOVE

Do research! Go online to collect some numerical data, such as sports scores. Create a box plot to summarize the data.

Choosing Measures to Describe Data

UNPACK THE STANDARD
You will choose which measurements to use when describing data.

LEARN IT: Sometimes, one measurement is better for describing a set of data than another. How can you tell?

Look at the first dot plot. The data is symmetrical. You can point to the middle. Both the median and mean are good measures here.

Look at the second dot plot. There are outliers. Outliers increase the mean. Think about how you find the mean: you add! If you are adding larger numbers, the mean will be bigger.

WAIT! Why does this matter?

Most of the data is clustered toward the left. The median will be in that data. It better describes this set. When picking measurements, make sure the ones you have will describe the majority of the data.

Example: The ages of the volunteers at a park clean-up project are shown. What measurement of center should you use? What about measurements of range?

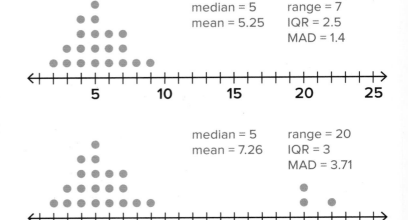

median = 5   range = 7
mean = 5.25   IQR = 2.5
               MAD = 1.4

median = 5   range = 20
mean = 7.26   IQR = 3
               MAD = 3.71

think! What other measures might describe these dot plots? Which measurements use mean and which use median? Can a measurement like MAD describe plot #2. Do you use mean to find the MAD?

Ages of Volunteers

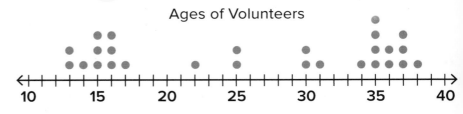

Step 1:	Step 2:	Step 3:
Describe the shape of the data.	Choose the better measure of center.	Choose the better measure of spread. *Hint:* IQR shows the spread of the middle of the data.
The data are clustered at both ends, with very little in the center.	There seem to be a similar number of data at either end. You can point toward the middle here—it is between the two data sets. You could use mean or median.	There aren't many points in the center. This means IQR will leave out most of the data. Range is a better choice because it measures the whole data set.

Standard: CCSS.Math.Content.6.SP.A.2, 6.SP.B.5c, 6.SP.B.5d

PRACTICE: Now you try

Choose the best measurements.

think!
How are the data
clustered?

1. What measure of center should you use? Why?

2. What measure of spread should you use? Why?

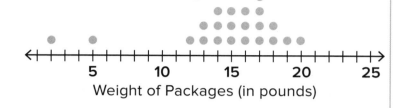

The hourly wages of employees at a department store are shown. Jamie says you cannot use MAD to describe the data. Do you agree with her? Why or why not? Show your work and explain your thinking on a piece of paper.

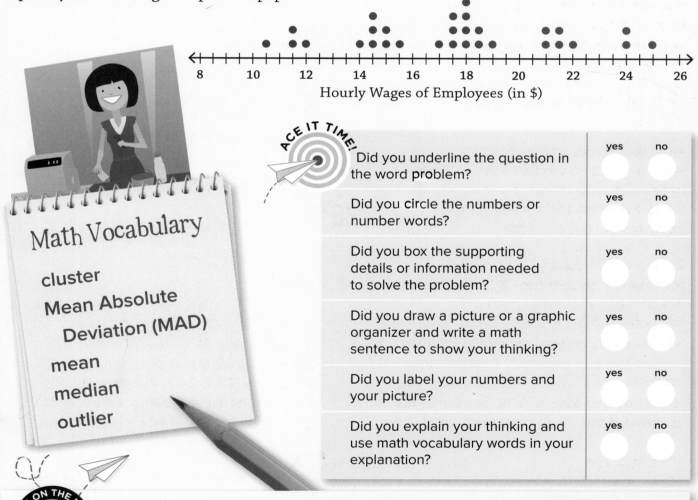

Math Vocabulary

cluster

Mean Absolute
   Deviation (MAD)

mean

median

outlier

ACE IT TIME!

	yes	no
Did you underline the question in the word **pro**blem?	◯	◯
Did you **ci**rcle the numbers or number words?	◯	◯
Did you box the supporting details or information needed to solve the problem?	◯	◯
Did you draw a picture or a graphic organizer and write a math sentence to show your thinking?	◯	◯
Did you label your numbers and your picture?	◯	◯
Did you explain your thinking and use math vocabulary words in your explanation?	◯	◯

MATH ON THE MOVE

Find 15 or more cans or boxes of food in your house. Choose a measure on the label, such as the grams of fiber or carbohydrates. Create a dot plot of the data. Explain which measures of center and variation would best describe the data and why.

REVIEW

Congratulations! You've finished the lessons for this unit. This means you've learned about statistics. You can recognize statistical questions. You know how to measure the center and variation of data. You have displayed and described data sets with dot plots, histograms, and box plots.

Now it's time to prove your skills with statistics. Solve the problems below! Use all of the methods you have learned.

Activity Section 1: Recognizing Statistical Questions

Which is the statistical question?

1. **A.** How old are the members of your school's student council?
   B. How old is the president of your school's student council?

2. **A.** How many apps did you download to your tablet last month?
   B. How many apps did your friends download to their tablets last month?

3. What is the difference between a statistical question and a non-statistical question?

Activity Section 2: Measures of Center

Solve the following problems.

1. Carolina's class is collecting donations to pay for their class trip to Washington, D.C. So far they have collected the following donations: $22, $35, $25, $15, $40, $25. What is the mean donation? What is the mode?

2. Darius competes on his school's track team. His 200-meter dash times are 23.8, 22.5, 22.6, 23.7, 24.2, 21.6, and 22.6 seconds. Find the mean, median, and mode of his times.

Standards: CCSS.Math.Content.6.SP.A.1, 6.SP.A.2, 6.SP.A.3, 6.SP.B.4, 6.SP.B.5a-d

Activity Section 3: Measures of Variation

Solve the following problems.

1. The high temperatures in San Diego, California for one week are 70, 74, 72, 81, 79, 76, and 80 degrees Fahrenheit.

   What is the range?

   What is the IQR of the temperatures?

2. Some students in Ms. Hall's class recorded these times in their reading log each day: 25, 27, 36, 34, 28, 22, 18, 30, and 33 minutes.

   What is the range?

   What is the IQR of the times?

Activity Section 4: Mean Absolute Deviation

Fill in the blanks.

1. Franco's bowling scores: 128, 166, 138, 154, 144

   mean =

   MAD =

2. Height, in inches, of a group of friends: 58, 47, 55, 65, 49, 63, 61, 58

   mean =

   MAD =

Activity Section 5: Dot Plots

Ava surveyed her classmates to see how many books they read last semester. She made a dot plot to display the data she collected.

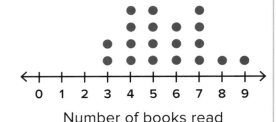

Number of books read

1. How many classmates did she survey?

2. What is the range?

3. What is the median?

4. What is the mean?

5. What is the mode?

6. Describe any patterns in the data.

Activity Section 6: Histograms

Use the histogram to answer questions 1–5.

1. How many phone calls are there in all?

2. Which time interval had the greatest number of phone calls?

3. How many phone calls were less than 12 minutes long?

4. How many phone calls were at least 18 minutes long?

5. In which interval is the median?

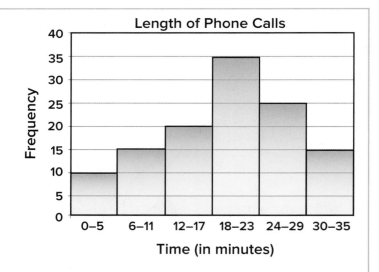

Standards: CCSS.Math.Content.6.SP.A.1, 6.SP.A.2, 6.SP.A.3, 6.SP.B.4, 6.SP.B.5a-d

Activity Section 7: Box Plots

The box plot shows the weights, in pounds, of puppies for sale at Furry Friends Pet Store.

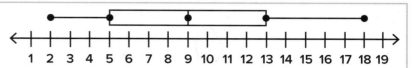

1. What is the range?

2. What is the median?

3. What is the interquartile range?

Activity Section 8: Choosing Measures to Describe Data

A group of sixth graders was asked how many texts they send each day. This dot plot is used to display the data.

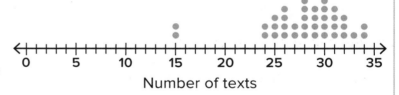

Number of texts

1. How are the data clustered? Does this affect the mean or median?

2. Which is the better measure of center—the mean or the median? Explain your choice.

3. Which is the better measure of variation—the range, the MAD, or the IQR? Explain your choice.

This dot plot shows the amount, in dollars, a group of sixth graders spent on lunch last week in the school cafeteria.

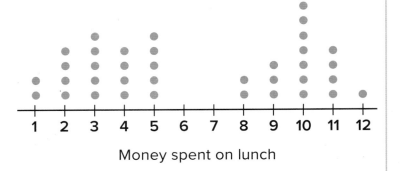

Money spent on lunch

4. How are the data clustered? Does this affect the mean or median?

5. Which is the better measure of center—the mean or the median? Explain your choice.

6. Which is the better measure of variation—the range, the MAD, or the IQR? Explain your choice.

Standards: CCSS.Math.Content.6.SP.A.1, 6.SP.A.2, 6.SP.A.3, 6.SP.B.4, 6.SP.B.5a-d

UNDERSTAND

Understand the meaning of what you have learned and apply your knowledge.

Use what you know about statistical measurements to answer the questions about the data set below.

Activity Section

Pythagorean Middle School hosts a Math and Science Family Night each spring. The attendance for the last 8 years was 98, 125, 103, 144, 165, 135, 148, and 154 people.

What is the range of the data set?

What is the median of the data set?

What is the interquartile range?

What is the mean of the data?

What is the mean absolute deviation?

DISCOVER

Discover how you can apply the information you have learned.

You can use box plots to summarize and describe a set of data. Box plots may only show five data points, but they can quickly tell us a lot of information about the data!

Activity Section

Kaia recorded the amount of time she studied for her science test in the last two weeks: 39, 45, 52, 67, 72, 76, and 55 minutes. As part of her homework, her teacher asked that she create a box plot to show the data. Kaia made this box plot, but there are some errors.

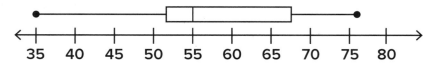

Draw the correct box plot:

Use the box plot you created to answer the following questions:

What is the median?

What is the lower quartile?

What is the upper quartile?

What is the interquartile range?

Standards: CCSS.Math.Content.6.SP.B.4, 6.SP.B.5c, CCSS.Math.Practice.MP1, MP2, MP3, MP4, MP5, MP6, MP7, MP8

Unit 2: CORE Ratio and Proportional Relationship Concepts

Understanding Ratios

Page 18 Practice: Now you try

1. Six to four, 6:4, $\frac{6}{4}$ OR Three to two, 3:2, $\frac{3}{2}$

2. Thirty-two to sixteen, 32:16, $\frac{32}{16}$ OR Two to one, 2:1, $\frac{2}{1}$

3. Sixteen to twenty-six, 16:26, $\frac{16}{26}$ OR Eight to thirteen, 8:13, $\frac{8}{13}$

4. Seventeen to forty, 17:40, $\frac{17}{40}$

5. Thirty-two to four, 32:4, $\frac{32}{4}$ OR Eight to one, 8:1, $\frac{8}{1}$

6. Six to two, 6:2, $\frac{6}{2}$ OR Three to one, 3:1, $\frac{3}{1}$

7. Part to part. Four to six, 4:6, $\frac{4}{6}$. (Answer requires only 1 form.)

8. Whole to part. Eight to two, 8:2, $\frac{8}{2}$. (Answer requires only 1 form.) You could also write four to one, 4:1, or $\frac{4}{1}$.

9. Part to part. Twenty-three to one, 23:1, $\frac{23}{1}$. (Answer requires only 1 form.)

10. Part to part. Two to three, 2:3, $\frac{2}{3}$. (Answer requires only 1 form.)

Page 19

Ace It Time: If there are 23 students and 14 like to play basketball, then 23 – 14 = 9 like to play volleyball.

Part to part ratio: 14:9 or 9:14. Answer should be written also in word form and as a fraction.

Part to whole: 14:23 or 9:23. Answer should be written also in word form and as a fraction.

Whole to part: 23:14 or 23:9. Answer should be written also in word form and as a fraction.

Understanding Unit Rates

Page 20 Practice: Now you try

1. Ratio: 18:2. Unit rate: $9 per book (9:1)

2. Ratio: 28:7. Unit rate: 4 miles per minute (4:1)

3. Ratio: 16:4. Unit rate: 4 strikes per minute (4:1)

4. Ratio: 92:4. Unit rate: 23 students per class (23:1)

Page 21

5. Marc pitched 5 strikeouts per game. (60:12 OR 5:1)

6. Ashlee rode her bike 2 miles per hour. (12:6 OR 2:1)

7. Miskha paid $5 per book. (40:8 OR 5:1)

8. It takes Grant 3 minutes per lap. (24:8 OR 3:1)

Ace It Time: Since it costs Julian $30 per 6 friends, this means it costs $5 per friend. (30:6 = 5:1) If he spends $40, then he can invite 8 friends because $\frac{\$40}{\$5}$ = 8 friends.

Double Number Lines and Equivalent Ratios

Page 23 Practice: Now you try

1. 18 liters

Juice (L)

Sparkling water (L)

2. 3 books

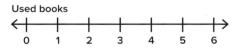

Used books

Cost ($)

Ace It Time: 12 lawns

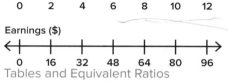

Lawns Mowed

Earnings ($)

Tables and Equivalent Ratios

Page 25 Practice: Now you try

1.

Number of feet	35	70	105	140
Number of minutes	1	2	3	4

2.

Number of pages	80	120	160	200
Number of books	2	3	4	5

3.

Number of apps	12	16	20	24
Number of folders	3	4	5	6

4.

Number of people	16	32	48	64
Number of games	4	8	12	16

5.

Number of boys	3	6	9	12
Number of girls	7	14	21	28

6.

Number of hours	4	8	12	16
Number of calls	13	26	39	52

Ace It Time:

Minutes	1	2	3	4	5
Sandwiches	4	8	12	16	20

Ordered Pairs:
(4, 1), (8, 2) (12, 3) (16, 4) (20, 5)

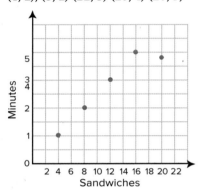

Understanding Unit Price and Constant Speed

Page 26 Practice: Now you try

1. It costs $0.65 per song vs. $0.90 per song. The first choice is a better deal.

2. It costs $0.40 per tennis ball vs. $0.25 per ball. The second choice is a better deal.

Page 27

3. It costs $3.25 per pound vs. $2.00 per pound. The second choice is a better deal.

4. It costs $3.60 per six-pack vs. $4.20 per six-pack. The first choice is a better deal.

5. 70 miles per hour

6. 1.5 pounds per week

7. 20 miles

8. 12 books

Ace It Time: The unit price of one cheeseburger at The Burger Hut is $1.25 per cheeseburger because $5.00 ÷ 4 = $1.25. The unit price of one cheeseburger at Big Burgers is $1.50 because $9.00 ÷ 6 = $1.50. I would rather eat at The Burger Hut because it is a better deal: $1.25 is less than $1.50.

Identifying Percent

Page 28 Practice: Now you try

1. $\frac{38}{100}$

2. $\frac{99}{100}$

3. $\frac{4}{100}$

Page 29

4. 16%

5. 7%

6. 80%

7. 46%

8. 35 people

9. 60% turquoise; 40% yellow

Ace It Time: Disagree; Horatio is incorrect. If there were 10 questions on his spelling quiz and he got 3 questions wrong, that means he got 7 out of 10 correct, or 70% correct.

Finding Percent of a Number

Page 31 Practice: Now you try

1. 450

2. 50

3. 6

4. 72

5. 180

6. 40

7. 60

8. 90

9. 80

Ace It Time: Cameron received $50.00 for his birthday. Use the expression 70% of n = $35, where "$n$" is the unknown amount of money he received for his birthday, or 0.70 × n = 35. Use division to solve: 35 ÷ 0.70 = 50. Check with multiplication:
$\frac{70}{100} \times \frac{50}{1} = \frac{3500}{100}$, or $\frac{35}{1}$, or $35.

Using Tape Diagrams with Percentages

Page 32 Practice: Now you try

1. 300

10%	20%	30%	40%	50%	60%	70%	80%	90%	100%
50	100	150	200	250	300	350	400	450	500

2. 105

10%	20%	30%	40%	50%	60%	70%	80%	90%	100%
15	30	45	60	75	90	105	120	135	150

Page 33

3. 120

10%	20%	30%	40%	50%	60%	70%	80%	90%	100%
30	60	90	120	150	180	210	240	270	300

4. 30

10%	20%	30%	40%	50%	60%	70%	80%	90%	100%
3	6	9	12	15	18	21	24	27	30

5. 60

10%	20%	30%	40%	50%	60%	70%	80%	90%	100%
6	12	18	24	30	36	42	48	54	60

Ace It Time: There are 110 sixth-graders in the whole school. 22 is 20% of 110. 22 ÷ 20% = 22 ÷ 0.20 = 110. Start the tape diagram at 20% with 22. 22 ÷ 2 = 11, so each box is worth 11. Keep counting by 11 until you get to 100%, or 110 total.

10%	20%	30%	40%	50%	60%	70%	80%	90%	100%
11	22	33	44	55	66	77	88	99	110

Ratios and Unit Conversions

Page 34 Practice: Now you try

1. 9 ft

2. 96 hrs

3. 4 gal

4. 7 cm

5. 8,000 g

6. 6,000 m

Page 35

7. <

8. =

9. >

10. >

11. <

12. <

13. 2.75 kg < 3,000 g; The laptop she uses at home is lighter.

14. 2 hr 15 min > 125 min; The 2 hr 15 min podcast is longer.

15. 5 times (200 m × 5 = 1,000 m = 1 km)

Ace It Time: Michaela can use the ratio 1:10 because 1 cm = 10 mm. Each bracelet uses 92 cm, or 92 × 10 = 920 mm. She needs 920 mm × 2 = 1,840 mm of twine to make both bracelets. She has 1,900 mm of twine. She has enough twine to make both bracelets because 1,900 > 1,840; she has more than she needs.

Unit 2 Stop and Think! Review

Page 36 Activity Section 1:

1. a. 3:4, or 3 to 4, or $\frac{3}{4}$ (accept any form of ratio)
   b. 4:3
   c. 3:2
   d. 2:4

2. a. 12:22
   b. 22:38
   c. 12:78
   d. 78:38

3. 12:32

4. 4:18

5. 9:5

Page 37 Activity Section 2:

1. $22.50 per shirt

2. $2.25 per pound

3. 18 miles per hour

4. 190 people per airplane

5. 4:2, or 2 eggs per 1 cup of milk

Page 38 Activity Section 3:

1. 4 songs for $5.00

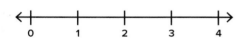

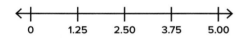

2. $48.00 for 6 hours of babysitting

Page 39 Activity Section 4:

1. 24, 40, 64

2. 12, 24, 48

3. 8, 16, 64

4. 8, 16, 24

5. a. 2, 4, 8, 10
   b. (1, 2), (2, 4), (3, 6), (4, 8), (5, 10)

c.

(Graph: Books read vs Months — points at (1,2), (2,4), (3,6), (4,8), (5,10))

6. D. $\frac{3}{8}$ is not equivalent to $\frac{3}{4}$. All of the other ratios are equivalent to $\frac{3}{4}$ because both the numerators and denominators are related to the numerator and denominator in $\frac{3}{4}$ either through multiplication or division.

Page 40 Activity Section 5:

1. $1.25 per pack

2. The unit price of each case is $7.00. 5 cases will cost $35.00.

3. 6 tubes of white paint

4. 4 minutes

5. Unit rate is 6 miles per hour; 24 miles in 4 hours

Activity Section 6:

1. 65%

2. 13%

3. 42%

4. 5%

5. 60%

6. 20%

7. $\frac{11}{100}$

8. $\frac{91}{100}$

9. $\frac{3}{100}$

10. $\frac{66}{100}$

Page 41 Activity Section 7:

1. 12

2. 14

3. 240

4. 150

5. 100

6. 300

7. 80 pieces

8. 9 movies

Activity Section 8:

1. 160

10%	20%	30%	40%	50%	60%	70%	80%	90%	100%
40	80	120	160	200	240	280	320	360	400

2. 90

10%	20%	30%	40%	50%	60%	70%	80%	90%	100%
15	30	45	60	75	90	105	120	135	150

3. 30

10%	20%	30%	40%	50%	60%	70%	80%	90%	100%
3	6	9	12	15	18	21	24	27	30

Page 42 Activity Section 9:

1. 6
2. 55,000
3. 15
4. 4
5. 20
6. 5
7. 4,000
8. 144
9. 55
10. 30
11. 2
12. 15,840
13. >
14. >
15. <
16. <
17. =
18. >
19. <
20. =
21. >
22. =
23. >
24. <

Unit 2 Stop and Think! Understand

Page 43 Activity Section:

The trip is 200 miles in total. If 80 miles = 40% of the total miles, then we can use division to solve. $\frac{80}{.40}$ = 200.

Unit 2 Stop and Think! Discover

Page 44 Activity Section:

1. 16, 24, 32

a. 8:1

b. 40 g of sugar

2. The ratio of carbohydrates to protein is 22:2 or 11:1. In 2 servings, there are 44 g of carbohydrates.

In 4 servings, there are 88 g of carbohydrates.

3. 4, 6, 8
4. 2:1
5. a. 30 g of fiber per day b. 5 servings

Unit 3: CORE Dividing Fractions Concepts
Dividing Fractions
Page 46 Practice: Now you try

1. 3
2. $\frac{4}{5}$
3. $1\frac{1}{5}$
4. $\frac{2}{3}$
5. $\frac{1}{4}$
6. 1
7. 6 burgers
8. 3 glasses

Page 47

Ace It Time: Leeza will have 5 pieces of ribbon because $\frac{5}{8} \div \frac{1}{8} = 5$.
$\frac{5}{8} \div \frac{1}{8} = \frac{5}{8} \times \frac{8}{1} = \frac{40}{8} = 5$

Dividing with Mixed Numbers
Page 48 Practice: Now you try

1. $1\frac{2}{5}$
2. $3\frac{1}{3}$
3. 3
4. $1\frac{3}{7}$
5. 2
6. $1\frac{2}{7}$

Page 49

7. $1\frac{1}{8}$ liters each
8. 3 pieces

Ace It Time: Mr. Elton will have 24 portions of clay because
$4\frac{4}{5} \div \frac{1}{5} = \frac{24}{5} \div \frac{1}{5} = \frac{24}{5} \times \frac{5}{1} = 24$.
He will have enough for the 22 students in his class because 24 > 22; he has more than he needs.

Unit 3 Stop and Think! Review
Page 50 Activity Section 1:

1. 3
2. $\frac{3}{4}$
3. $1\frac{1}{2}$
4. 4
5. $1\frac{1}{8}$
6. $\frac{1}{3}$

7. 3 bags
8. $\frac{1}{8}$ quart = $\frac{1}{2}$ cup
9. 6 runners

Page 51

10. $\frac{1}{2}$. You know $\frac{1}{2}$ is the reciprocal because $2 \times \frac{1}{2} = 1$. Multiplying by reciprocals should give you 1.

11. To solve $\frac{3}{4} \div \frac{1}{3}$, first convert the divisor ($\frac{1}{3}$) to its reciprocal ($\frac{3}{1}$). Multiply the dividend by the reciprocal. $\frac{3}{4} \times \frac{3}{1} = \frac{9}{4}$. Lastly, you have to simplify. $\frac{9}{4} = 2\frac{1}{4}$.

12. C. Asking how many servings is asking how many $\frac{3}{4}$ parts fit into $2\frac{2}{3}$ cups of yogurt. To find the number of parts in a whole, you divide. Since you are finding the number of $\frac{3}{4}$ cup servings in $2\frac{2}{3}$ cups of yogurt, you divide the whole ($2\frac{2}{3}$) by the part ($\frac{3}{4}$).

Page 52 Activity Section 2:

1. 14
2. $2\frac{1}{3}$
3. 3
4. 2
5. 15
6. $5\frac{3}{5}$
7. $\frac{1}{2}$ meter
8. 8 pieces
9. 10 scoops
10. The width is 2 km. $A = l \times w$, or $1\frac{1}{2} = \frac{3}{4} \times$ width. We can use division to solve:
$1\frac{1}{2} \div \frac{3}{4} = \frac{3}{2} \div \frac{3}{4} = \frac{3}{2} \times \frac{4}{3} = \frac{12}{6} = 2$.

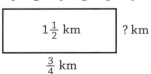

Unit 3 Stop and Think! Understand
Page 53 Activity Section:

Joel has 3 pieces to fix his treehouse. First, he started with a board that was $\frac{5}{6}$-yard long. If he cut off $\frac{1}{3}$ yard because of damage, he had
$\frac{5}{6} - \frac{1}{3} = \frac{5}{6} - \frac{2}{6} = \frac{3}{6} = \frac{1}{2}$ yard left. (To do the subtraction, use common denominators.) Next, to find how many $\frac{1}{6}$ pieces Joel cut, divide
$\frac{1}{2} \div \frac{1}{6} = \frac{1}{2} \times \frac{6}{1} = \frac{6}{2} = 3$.

Unit 3 Stop and Think! Discover
Page 54 Activity Section:

Jeremy is correct because Dione stopped 3 times, which is greater than the 2 times he stopped. To find the number of times Dione stopped, divide and use reciprocals:
$3\frac{3}{4} \div 1\frac{1}{4} = \frac{15}{4} \div \frac{5}{4} = \frac{15}{4} \times \frac{4}{5} = \frac{60}{20} = 3$.

Unit 4: CORE Number System Operation Concepts
Division Review
Page 56 Practice: Now you try

1. 32 r1
2. 102 r41
3. 319 r4
4. 120 r4
5. 27 cellphones
6. 21 napkin holders

Page 57

Ace It Time: The snack food company will be able to fill 370 16-ounce packages because 5,929 ÷ 16 = 370 r9. If we interpret the remainder of 9, that is not enough dried fruit snacks to fill another package, so we drop the remainder. To check with multiplication, multiply the quotient by the divisor and add the remainder:
370 × 16 + 9 = 5,929.

Adding Decimals
Page 58 Practice: Now you try

1. 201.847
2. 143.74
3. 19.05
4. 14.60
5. 296.251
6. 864.778
7. $7.74
8. 977.82 miles

Page 59

Ace It Time: By the end of the third week, Ricardo's plant measured 8.726 cm tall.
4.576 + 1.7 + 2.45 = 8.726. I added the decimals by lining up the decimal point, even though one decimal was written to the tenths place, one written to the hundredths place, and one written to the thousandths place.

Subtracting Decimals

Page 60 Practice: Now you try

1. 42.413
2. 10.705
3. 0.485 points
4. 1.395 kilometers
5. 76.776
6. 380.094
7. 17.355 gallons
8. $1.72

Page 61

Ace It Time: Evelyn is not correct. The correct answer is 6.25 − 2.0 = 4.25. Evelyn incorrectly lined up her decimal points, and solved the problem as 6.25 − .20 = 6.05.

Multiplying Decimals

Page 63 Practice: Now you try

1. 11.745
2. 7.71
3. 63.896
4. $3.68
5. $21.25

Ace It Time: Viola is correct; she spent less than $5.00 on the cherries because 2.5 × 1.99 = 4.975. Since we are working with money, we round that decimal to the nearest hundredths place, or $4.98, which is less than $5.00.

Dividing Decimals

Page 64 Practice: Now you try

1. 17.3
2. 4.56
3. 34.5
4. 12 rides
5. $3.35 per gallon
6. 200.75
7. 8.6
8. 20.5

Page 65

Ace It Time: Sasha earned $5.50 per hour because
2.5 hours a day × 3 days = 7.5 total hours.
$41.25 ÷ 7.5 hours = $5.50 per hour.

Greatest Common Factors

Page 67 Practice: Now you try

1. 9: 1, 3, 9
   24: 1, 2, 3, 4, 6, 8, 12, 24
   GCF = 3
2. 14: 1, 2, 7, 14
   28: 1, 2, 4, 7, 14, 28
   GCF = 14
3. 16: 1, 2, 4, 8, 16
   40: 1, 2, 4, 5, 8, 10, 20, 40
   GCF = 8
4. 15: 1, 3, 5, 15
   60: 1, 2, 3, 4, 5, 6, 10, 12, 15, 20, 30, 60
   GCF = 15
5. 25: 1, 5, 25
   45: 1, 3, 5, 9, 15, 45
   GCF = 5
6. 36: 1, 2, 3, 4, 6, 9, 12, 18, 36
   48: 1, 2, 3, 4, 6, 8, 12, 16, 24, 48
   GCF = 12
7. GCF = 8
   $(8 \times 2) + (8 \times 3) = 8(2 + 3) = 8(5) = 40$
8. GCF = 25
   $(25 \times 2) + (25 \times 3) = 25 (2+3) = 25(5) = 125$
9. GCF = 7
   $(7 \times 8) + (7 \times 5) = 7(8 + 5) = 7(13) = 91$

Ace It Time: Tamara can make 7 gift bags because 7 is the greatest common factor (GCF) of 35 and 28. If she has 35 pencils to fill 7 bags, then she will have 5 pencils in each bag (35 ÷ 7 = 5.) If she has 28 erasers and 7 bags, then she will have 4 erasers in each bag (28 ÷ 7 = 4).

Least Common Multiples

Page 69 Practice: Now you try

1. 24
2. 10
3. 36
4. 36
5. 60
6. 24
7. 40 hot dogs and 40 buns (or 4 packages of hot dogs, and 5 packages of buns)
8. 12 apples and 12 oranges (or 3 bags of apples, and 2 bags of oranges)

Ace It Time: Ezra's method will give a common multiple, but it won't always give the least common multiple. Using this method, if you multiply 5 × 6 = 30, you get the LCM for 5 and 6. It does NOT work for 5 and 10 because 5 × 10 = 50, but the LCM of these two numbers is 10. So Ezra's method does not always work to find the LCM.

Unit 4 Stop and Think! Review

Page 70 Activity Section 1:

1. 150 r25
2. 20 r14
3. 332 r52
4. 37 bookshelves
5. 82 classrooms

Page 71 Activity Section 2:

1. 132.08
2. 386.849
3. 687.699
4. 8.85 mL
5. 11.9 km

Activity Section 3:

1. 63.695
2. 400.39
3. 580.97
4. $28.64
5. $6.52

Page 72 Activity Section 4:

1. 288.804
2. 2.534
3. 12,249.60
4. 1.98 meters
5. 2.375 miles

Activity Section 5:

1. 137.8
2. 352
3. 13.6
4. 5 songs
5. $5.50 per hour

Page 73 Activity Section 6:

1. 8: 1, 2, 4, 8
   28: 1, 2, 4, 7, 14, 28
   GCF: 4
2. 5: 1,5
   20: 1, 2, 4, 5, 10, 20
   GCF: 5

3. 16: 1, 2, 4, 8, 16
   32: 1, 2, 4, 8, 16, 32
   GCF: 16

4. 12: 1, 2, 3, 4, 6, 12
   72: 1, 2, 3, 4, 6, 8, 9, 12, 18, 24, 36, 72
   GCF: 12

5. 18: 1, 2, 3, 6, 9, 18
   45: 1, 3, 5, 9, 15, 45
   GCF: 9

6. 20: 1, 2, 4, 5, 10, 20
   60: 1, 2, 3, 4, 5, 6, 10, 12, 15, 20, 30, 60
   GCF: 20

7. GCF = 5
   (5 × 6) + (5 × 9) = 5(6 + 9)
   5(15) = 75

8. GCF = 6
   (6 × 2) + (6 × 6) = 6(2 + 6) = 6(8) = 48

9. GCF = 9
   (9 × 4) + (9 × 3) = 9(4 + 3) = 9(7) = 63

Activity Section 7:

1. 8: 8, 16, 24, 32, 40...
   12: 12, 24, 36...
   LCM: 24

2. 2: 2, 4, 6, 8, 10, 12, 14...
   7: 7, 14, 21...
   LCM: 14

3. 9: 9, 18, 27, 36, 45...
   6: 6, 12, 18, 24, 30, 36...
   LCM: 18

4. 2: 2, 4, 6, 8, 10, 12, 14, 16, 18, 20...
   20: 20, 40, 60...
   LCM: 20

5. 5: 5, 10, 15, 20, 25...
   10: 10, 20, 30...
   LCM: 10

6. 3: 3, 6, 9, 12, 15...
   4: 4, 8, 12, 16...
   LCM: 12

Unit 4 Stop and Think! Understand
Page 74 Activity Section:

1. 3 and 5

2. 2, 4, 12

3. 5 and 30

4. Answers will vary, but should result in two numbers that share a GCF

5. Answers will vary, but should result in two numbers that share an LCM

Unit 4 Stop and Think! Discover
Page 75 Activity Section:

One T-shirt at The Closet costs $7.84.

To find this, first calculate the cost of 4 T-shirts at Wear It: 4 × $9.80 = $39.20. Since 5 T-shirts at The Closet cost the same amount, divide by 5 to find the unit price at The Closet: $39.20 ÷ 5 = $7.84.

Coral is right. The Closet offers the better deal because it has a cheaper unit price. $7.84 < $9.80.

Unit 5: CORE Rational Number Concepts

Understanding Integers
Page 76 Practice: Now you try

1. −8

2. +17

3. −54

4. +104

Page 77

5. +40

6. −2

7. −13

8. +1

9. −7

10. −15

Ace It Time: Micah is incorrect. A decrease of 5,000 points is −5,000, not +5,000. Losing points is a negative action.

Graphing Integers on a Number Line
Page 78 Practice: Now you try

1. −4

2. +7

3. +9

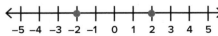

4. −2

Page 79

5. 14

6. 48

7. 5

8. −105

9. −15

10. 1

Ace It Time:

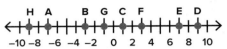

A = −7, B = −3, C = +1, D = +9

E = +7, F = +3, G = −1, H = −9

Comparing and Ordering Integers
Page 80 Practice: Now you try

1. −8 < −4

2. −1 > −2

Page 81

3. >

4. <

5. >

6. −15, −14, −13, −12

7. −2, −1, 1, 2

8. −17, −11, −7, −5

Ace It Time: The record temperature in Alaska of −80 degrees F is colder than the record of −70 degrees F in Montana. Both degrees are negative integers, but −80 is farther from zero than −70. This can be shown on a vertical number line, and can also be written as the inequality −80 < −70.

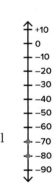

Ordering Rational Numbers
Page 82 Practice: Now you try

1. $-\frac{3}{4} < -\frac{1}{2}$

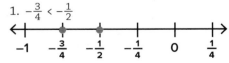

2. $-0.25 > -\frac{2}{4}$

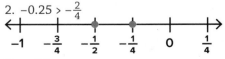

Page 83

3. >

4. >

5. <

6. <

7. >

8. <

Ace It Time: From coldest to warmest, the temperatures are −60.24°C, −45.25°C, −36.8°C, −36$\frac{1}{4}$°C. To compare, first convert the fraction to a decimal: −36$\frac{1}{4}$°C = −36.25°C. Compare the decimals.

Understanding Absolute Value
Page 84 Practice: Now you try

1. 44

2. 81

3. 7$\frac{3}{5}$

4. 20.5

5. 3$\frac{1}{3}$

6. 45.25

Page 85

7. $25.50

8. 32

9. 42,000

Ace It Time: Juan is correct. Even though −40 > −45, the absolute values show that |−45| > |−40|. Since −45 is farther from zero, it means more money has been lost.

Comparing With and Without Absolute Value
Page 87 Practice: Now you try

1. Carmen has more than $3 of debt. |−5| > |3|

2. They lost more yards on the 15-yard play. |15| > |−10|

3. Greg has the lowest score. −10 < −5 < −2

4. Lake Erie is shallower. |−210| < |−278|

Ace It Time: Answers will vary, but all numbers should be greater than |−24|. Numbers like 25, 26, and |−27| are all correct. Numbers in between −24 and 24 are all incorrect, whether or not you include absolute value signs.

Ordered Pairs on a Coordinate Plane
Page 89 Practice: Now you try

1. I

2. II

3. IV

4. III

5. y-axis

6. x-axis

7–12. See coordinate plane:

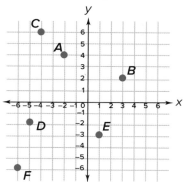

Ace It Time: Jonah is incorrect because the ordered pair (4, −4) is located in Quadrant IV. The x-coordinate (4) tells us to go 4 units to the right on the x-axis. The y-coordinate (−4) tells us to go 4 units down on the y-axis.

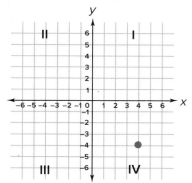

Graphing Integers and Rational Numbers
Page 90 Practice: Now you try

1–8.

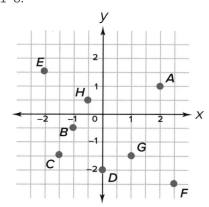

9–12. Answers will vary

Page 91

Ace It Time: Point D is located at the ordered pair (3$\frac{1}{2}$, −1$\frac{1}{2}$). Points A and B are reflections across the y-axis. Points A and C are reflections across the x-axis. To make a rectangle, point D must be a reflection of points B and C.

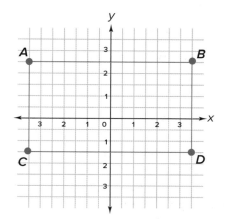

Graphing and Finding Distance on Coordinate Planes
Page 93 Practice: Now you try

1. 1 unit

2. 5 units

3. 7 units

4. 5 units

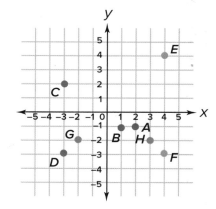

Ace It Time: Rifi is incorrect. The distance between (2, −6) and (−6, −6) is 8 units. This is found by graphing and counting units, or by adding absolute values.

$$|2| + |−6| = 2 + 6 = 8$$

Answer Key

Page 94 Activity Section 1:

1. +44
2. −3
3. +121
4. −18
5. −3
6. +15
7. +500
8. +40
9. −23
10. −20

Activity Section 2:

1. −1

2. +9

3. +6

4. −2

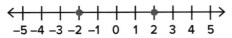

Page 95

5. 23
6. 17
7. 8
8. −45
9. −34
10. 11

Activity Section 3:

1. −6 > −7

2. −9 < −6

3. >
4. >
5. <
6. −2, −12, −21, −22
7. 4, 3, −3, −4
8. −86, −88, −89, −90

Activity Section 4:

1. $-0.25 > -\frac{1}{2}$

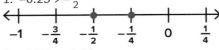

2. −0.75 < −0.50

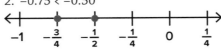

3. −2.5, −2.40, −2.35, −2.25
4. $-1, -\frac{3}{4}, -\frac{1}{2}, -\frac{1}{4}$
5. $-3\frac{1}{2}, -3\frac{1}{4}, -3.20, -3.15$
6. $-1.75, -1.5, -1\frac{1}{4}, -1\frac{1}{5}$

Page 96 Activity Section 5:

1. 14
2. 72
3. $5\frac{3}{8}$
4. 36.25
5. $4\frac{7}{8}$
6. 24.35
7. $45.00
8. 22
9. 13,000

Activity Section 6:

1. Kamal's debt is greater than $10.
$|-\$12| > |\$10|$
2. Chloe has the higher score. She has
10 − 29 = −19. −19 > −20

Activity Section 7:

1. IV
2. I
3. III
4. III
5. *y*-axis
6. *x*-axis

Page 97 Activity Section:

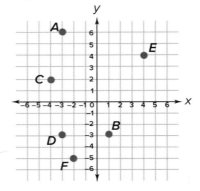

7. II
8. IV
9. II
10. III
11. I
12. III

Activity Section 8:

1–8.

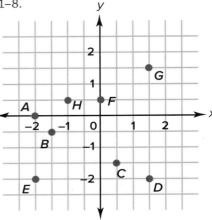

Activity Section 9:

1. 10 units
2. 6 units
3. 2 units
4. 3 units
5. One way to find the distance between two coordinate points is to graph both points on a coordinate grid and count the number of units between them. Another way is to add the absolute values of the different coordinates if they are in different quadrants or subtract the absolute values of the different coordinates if they are in the same quadrant.

Page 98 Activity Section:

From warmest to coldest, the temperatures were: 3.3°F, −2.3°F, −2.45°F, and −3.2°F. Darius is incorrect. The 6 AM temperature of −3.2°F is the coldest temperature because it is the lowest temperature. It is furthest from 0. −3.2 < −2.45

Unit 5 Stop and Think! Discover
Page 99 Activity Section:

Point	Reflection
A (−5, −2)	E **(−5, 2)**
B (−3, −2)	F **(−3, 2)**
C (−3, −5)	G **(−3, 5)**
D (−5, −5)	H **(−5, 5)**

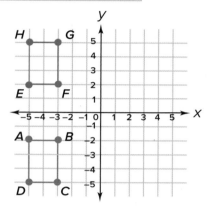

Unit 6: CORE Expression Concepts

Numerical Expressions with Exponents
Page 101 Practice: Now you try

1. 47
2. 11
3. 54
4. 4
5. 12
6. 25
7. 23
8. 11

Ace It Time: To find the value of an expression, simplify it by following the Order of Operations.

$$(2 \div 2) + 2 \times 2^2 - 2$$

First, solve what is inside the parentheses:

$$1 + 2 \times 2^2 - 2$$

Then solve the exponents:

$$1 + 2 \times 4 - 2$$

Then multiply from left to right:

$$1 + 8 - 2$$

Then add and subtract from left to right: 7

Writing Expressions
Page 102 Practice: Now you try

1. $y - 32$
2. $45 \div m$
3. $f + 102$
4. $18z$
5. $36 \div g + 5$
6. $7n - 2$

Page 103

7. $b + 3$
8. $6a$
9. $9t + 20p$
10. $2p - 5$

Ace It Time: Julius is wrong because he used the wrong operation. The price of graphic novels is $12n$ and the price of bookmarks is $3b$. To find the total price, you add the amount together instead of multiplying: $12n + 3b$. That's what the "and" means in the sentence, "Julius buys n graphic novels at \$12 each *and* 3 bookmarks at \$$b$ each."

Identifying Parts of Expressions
Page 105 Practice: Now you try

1. $2x$ and $(6 - 1)$; 2
2. (3×4) and $8n$; 8
3. 12 times the quotient of 45 and 9
4. 4 times a minus 2 times b
5. 45 plus the product of 8 and 5
6. 8 times the difference of 9.5 and 3.6
7. 60 divided by the sum of 5.5 and 4.5
8. The product of 2.1 and 3.45 minus 6.5

Ace It Time: The expression $3 \times (3 + 12)$ has two terms: the number 3 and the sum of $3 + 12$. The expression $3 \times 3 + 12$ has three terms: the numbers 3, 3, and 12.
$3 \times (3 + 12)$ can be written as "3 times the sum of 3 and 12."
$3 \times 3 + 12$ can be written as "3 times 3 plus 12."

Evaluating Expressions
Page 106 Practice: Now you try

1. 22
2. 5

3. 56
4. 18
5. 13.9
6. 36

Page 107

7. 12
8. 14
9. 15
10. 60
11. 16
12. 26.05

Ace It Time: Tyrel is correct. If the volume of a cube is l × w × h, and the size of each side of the cube is s, then you can substitute s into the expression. l × w × h becomes $s \times s \times s$, which is the same as s^3.
The volume of the cube if $s = 3$ is 3^3 cubic units. Simplified, this is 27 cubic units.

Generating Equivalent Expressions
Page 108 Practice: Now you try

1. $5d$
2. $4x + 6y$
3. $13 + 3x$
4. $5r$
5. $18g - 2h$
6. $6y$

Page 109

7. $4m + 48$
8. $96 + 12p$
9. $4(s - t)$
10. $6a + 18b$
11. $3.5w + 7$
12. $\frac{1}{2}s + 5$

Ace It Time: A square has four equal sides. To find the perimeter of this square, add the length of the four sides: $4s + 4s + 4s + 4s$. Equivalent expressions could be $4 \times 4s$ or $16s$.

Identifying Equivalent Expressions
Page 110 Practice: Now you try

1. True
2. True
3. False
4. True

Page 111

5. $(6 \times 3) + 6x$ or $18 + 6x$
6. $(3 \times 2c) - 3d$ or $6c - 3d$
7. $5m$

Answer Key

8. $4(8s + 3t)$
9. p^2
10. $5(3k - 2j)$

Ace It Time: Carolina is wrong. $8t \times 6$ is NOT equivalent to $14t$. She incorrectly used the Distributive Property to write $(8 + 6)t$, which simplifies to $14t$. An equivalent expression for $8t \times 6$ is $48t$. You can get this using the Commutative Property. $8 \times t \times 6 = 8 \times 6 \times t = 48t$. Another equivalent expression using the GCF is $2(4t \times 3)$.

More Work with Writing Expressions
Page 112 Practice: Now you try
1. a. $2c + 1$
   b. $2(1\frac{1}{2}) + 1 = 4$ cups

Page 113
2. a. $(36 - 3)c$ or $33c$
   b. $33(6) = 198$ tomatoes
3. a. $25 + 0.10t$
   b. $25 + 0.10(12) = \$26.20$
4. a. $46 + 9s$
   b. $46 + 9(4) = \$82.00$

Ace It Time: Jim is 28 years old. The expression that shows Jim's age is $4 + 2k$. To solve for Jim's age, substitute 12 for the variable. Use the Order of Operations to simplify.

$$4 + 2(12)$$
$$4 + 24$$
$$28$$

Unit 6 Stop and Think! Review
Page 114 Activity Section 1:
1. 8
2. 17
3. 4
4. 68
5. 13
6. 21
7. 14
8. 12

Activity Section 2:
1. $g + 12$
2. $x - 18$
3. $\frac{y}{4}$
4. $2n$
5. $\frac{42}{t} - 4$
6. $12x + 3$
7. $12 + n$
8. $2t + 5$

9. $18 + 12b$
10. $6(5 + c)$ OR $30 + 6c$

Page 115 Activity Section 3:
1. $(4 + 3)$ and $4n$; 4
2. $(12x + 2)$ and (5×3); 12
3. 3 times the sum of 7 and 5
4. 4 times z minus 3 times y
5. 20 divided by the product of 2 times 2
6. 2 times b plus 3 times 2

Activity Section 4:
1. 15
2. 7
3. 12
4. 59
5. 9
6. 10.08
7. 29
8. 6
9. 43
10. 11
11. 360
12. 17.9

Page 116 Activity Section 5:
1. $3f$
2. $8g + 12$
3. $12 - 2v$
4. $48 + 9y$
5. p^2
6. $8m + 3$
7. $6k + 12$
8. $8 + 4v$
9. $7.5t + 22.5$
10. $4x + 8y$
11. $\frac{r}{2} + 6$
12. $12g$

Activity Section 6:
1. $12v + 72$
2. $48m$
3. $16 - 2w$
4. $8(5a - 3b)$
5. $3g + 18$
6. $4(3j + 8k)$

Page 117 Activity Section 7:
1. a. $18p$
   b. 72 apartments
2. a. $2(4 + a)$ OR $8 + 2a$
   b. 20 apps
3. a. $4.50 + 2s$
   b. $12.50
4. a. $44 + 10n$
   b. $104

Unit 6 Stop and Think! Understand
Page 118 Activity Section:
One expression for the longer shelf is $4(4.6a + 3)$. An equivalent expression can be found using the Distributive Property: $18.4a + 12$.

Unit 6 Stop and Think! Discover
Page 119 Activity Section:
Johanna is correct. Use the expression $1.8C + 32$ to convert the temperature in the Bahamas to Fahrenheit: $1.8(31) + 32 = 87.8$. The temperature in the Bahamas was 87.8°C. If the temperature back home in Michigan was 86°F, it was hotter in the Bahamas because $87.8 > 86$.

Unit 7: CORE Equation Concepts
Solving Equations
Page 120 Practice: Now you try
1. $x = 38$; $6 + 38 = 44$
2. $y = 37$; $37 - 12 = 25$
3. $n = 6$; $7 \times 6 = 42$
4. $a = 36$; $36 \div 3 = 12$
5. $c = 340$; $975 = 340 + 635$
6. $s = 672$; $\frac{672}{6} = 112$

Page 121
Ace It Time: Mari is 48 inches tall. The equation for this problem is $m + 16 = 64$, where m = Mari's height. The inverse operation of addition is subtraction. Solving using subtraction gives $m = 48$. *Note: This problem can also be solved by using the equation $64 - 16 = m$, but that wouldn't require an inverse operation to solve.*

Solving Equations in Real-World Contexts
Page 122 Practice: Now you try
1. $y + 4 = 9$; $y = 5$ years
2. $20d = 360$; $d = 18$ days
3. $d + 17 = 76$; $d = 59$ degrees
4. $4f = 72$; $f = 18$ feet

Page 123
5. $p + 8 = 91$; $p = 83$ points
6. $36c = 432$; $c = 12$ cleats

Ace It Time: Anthony started with $1\frac{1}{2}$ cups of milk in the carton. Use the equation $m - \frac{5}{8} = \frac{7}{8}$, where m represents how much milk was in the carton when Anthony started cooking. Use the inverse operation of subtraction (addition) to solve.

$$\frac{7}{8} + \frac{5}{8} = m$$
$$\frac{12}{8} = m$$

Remember to simplify!

$$\frac{12}{8} = 1\frac{4}{8} = 1\frac{1}{2} \text{ cups of milk}$$

Writing Inequalities

Page 124 Practice: Now you try

1. $n > 4$
2. $n \le 5$

Page 125

3. $n \le 25$
4. $n \ge 48$
5. True
6. False
7. True
8. $n < 6$
9. $n \ge -7$

Ace It Time: Chrystal has $p \ge 60$ photos saved to her computer. We know this because the number of photos (p) is 3 times the number of songs on her computer. She has at least 20 songs. This means she has at least 3×20 photos. We use the greater than or equal sign because she has "at least" that many. This means she could have 20 songs or she could have more; she could have 3×20 photos or she could have more. If $p \ge 3 \times 20$ photos, then $p \ge 60$ photos. You could also write this as $\frac{p}{3} \ge 20$. This is the same as doing the opposite operation to both sides of the inequality.

Solving Inequalities

Page 126 Practice: Now you try

1. 60, 70
2. 13, 12, 11
3. 10, 12
4. 3, 4, 5

Page 127

5. True
6. False
7. False
8. True

Ace It Time: The inequality $a + 6 \ge 18$ does describe the possible ages of Jocelyn's classmates. The numbers in the solution set that make the inequality true are 12 and 13. You can tell by substituting each number in the solution set for the variable a to see if it

makes the inequality true.

$10 + 6 \ge 18$ is NOT true
$11 + 6 \ge 18$ is NOT true
$12 + 6 \ge 18$ is true
$13 + 6 \ge 18$ is true

Independent and Dependent Variables

Page 128 Practice: Now you try

1. 6; Independent: x; Dependent: y; Equation: $y = x + 2$
2. 5; Independent: y; Dependent: z; Equation: $z = y - 3$

Page 129

3. 10.50; Independent: b; Dependent: c; Equation: $c = 3.50b$
4. 48; Independent: c; Dependent: p; Equation: $c = 16p$

Ace It Time:

Months (m)	Books (b)
1	3
2	6
3	9
4	12
5	15

Independent variable: m (months)
Dependent variable: b (books)
Equation: $b = 3m$
The amount of books Kayleigh reads depends on how many months she has been reading. This means b is the dependent variable, and m is the independent variable.

Graphing Independent and Dependent Variables

Page 130 Practice: Now you try

1. $y = 3x$

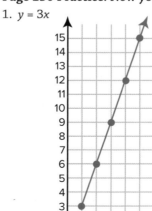

2. $y = 2x - 1$

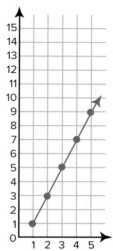

Page 131

Ace It Time: Keiser made an error by graphing the wrong variables on the x- and y-axes. The years (y) are the independent variable in this problem and should be graphed on the horizontal x-axis. The money (x) is the dependent variable and should be graphed on the vertical y-axis. Just because the variable y is used for years, does not mean it is the y variable.

Unit 7 Stop and Think! Review

Page 132 Activity Section 1:

1. $x = 51$; $13 + 51 = 64$
2. $n = 90$; $9(90) = 810$
3. $a = 49$; $49 \div 7 = 7$
4. $z = 84$; $84 - 22 = 62$
5. $y = 47$; $159 = 47 + 112$
6. $t = 512$; $\frac{512}{4} = 128$

Page 133 Activity Section 2:

Equations and letters used for variables may vary.

1. $24 \div c = 6$; $c = 4$ children
2. $4p = 88$; $p = 22$ pages
3. $78 + 5 = t$; $t = 83$ degrees
4. $12n = 60$; $n = 5$ lawns
5. $14b = 112$; $b = 8$ boxes
6. $120 = 3s$; $s = 40$ sit-ups

Page 134 Activity Section 3:

Letters used for variables may vary.

1. $t > 2$
2. $b \le 3$
3. $m \le 15$
4. $a \ge 5$

5. False
6. False
7. True
8. False
9. True
10. True
11. $n > -1$
12. $n \leq 5$

Activity Section 4:

1. 40
2. 6, 7
3. $\frac{1}{4}$, 1, $1\frac{1}{4}$, 2
4. 6, 9, 12
5. False
6. False
7. True
8. True
9. False
10. True

Page 135 Activity Section 5:

1.

Months (m)	Number of books (c)
1	2
2	4
3	6
4	8

Equation: $b = 2m$
Independent variable: m
Dependent variable: b

2.

Number of shoes (s)	Total cost (b)
1	12
2	24
3	36
4	48

Equation: $c = 12s$
Independent variable: s
Dependent variable: c

3.

x	y
1	5
2	6
3	7
4	8

Equation: $y = x + 4$
Independent variable: x
Dependent variable: y

4.

x	y
5	2.5
6	3
7	3.5
8	4

Equation: $x = 2y$
Independent variable: y
Dependent variable: x

Page 136 Activity Section 6:

1.

Number of Sundaes (s)	Total Cost (c)
1	6
2	12
3	18
4	24
5	30

Ordered pairs: (1,6), (2,12), (3,18), (4,24), (5,30)
Equation: $c = 6s$

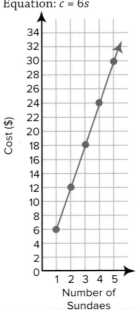

Unit 7 Stop and Think! Understand
Page 137 Activity Section:

Input (x)	Output (y)
3	1
6	2
9	3
12	4
15	5

Rule: **Divide** the input variable by **3** to get the output variable.
Equation: **$y = x \div 3$**

Unit 7 Stop and Think! Discover
Page 138 Activity Section:

Gabriel is correct. The equation $t = 22j + 8$ calculates the total cost for the jerseys ($22j$) and includes the shipping cost (8). Damon's equation $t = 22j + 8j$ is the same as $t = (22 + 8)j$ or $t = 30j$. This incorrectly adds an $8 shipping fee for each shirt, instead of one fee for the whole order.

Unit 8: CORE Geometry Concepts

Area of Triangles and Quadrilaterals
Page 140 Practice: Now you try

1. 19.38 cm²
2. $19\frac{1}{2}$ in.²
3. 139.5 cm²
4. 180 ft²
5. 120 yd²
6. 96 m²

Page 141

Ace It Time: Since the banner has four sides with one pair of parallel sides, it is a trapezoid. The area is 21 feet². Use the formula $A = \frac{1}{2}(b_1 + b_2)h$. Substitute the values of $base_1$, $base_2$, and the height.

$$A = \frac{1}{2}(4 + 8)3.5$$
$$= \frac{1}{2}(12)3.5$$
$$= 21$$

Area of Composite Figures
Page 142 Practice: Now you try

1. 45 ft²
2. 60 m²
3. 20 m²

4. 184 in.²

Page 143

Ace It Time: 1,140 ft² of carpeting is needed. The floor can be divided into a parallelogram with base 30 ft and height 26 ft and a right triangle with height 24 ft and base 30 ft.

A of parallelogram

$$= 30 \times 26$$
$$= 780 \text{ ft}^2$$

A of triangle $= \frac{1}{2}(24 \times 30)$
$$= 360 \text{ ft}^2$$

A of floor = 780 + 360 = 1,140 ft²

Volume of Rectangular Prisms

Page 144 Practice: Now you try

1. 50 in.³

2. $42\frac{7}{8}$ ft³

3. $527\frac{1}{4}$ ft³

4. $1\frac{2}{3}$ yd³

Page 145

5. 186 in.³

6. $5\frac{1}{4}$ ft³

Ace It Time: Chloe's cooler can hold $3\frac{3}{8}$ cubic feet of ice. A cube has equal length, width, and height, so
$V = 1\frac{1}{2} \times 1\frac{1}{2} \times 1\frac{1}{2} = \frac{27}{8} = 3\frac{3}{8}$ feet³.

Polygons on the Coordinate Plane

Page 146 Practice: Now you try

1. Point $J = (-2, 1)$
   Length of side KL = 2 units
   Length of side ML = 5 units

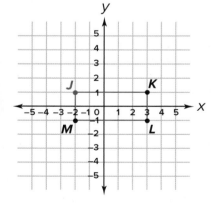

2. Point $F = (0, -2)$
   Length of side CD = 3 units
   Length of side FE = 3 units

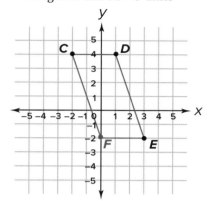

Page 147

3. Trapezoid
   Length of side DE = 5 units
   Length of side GF = 9 units

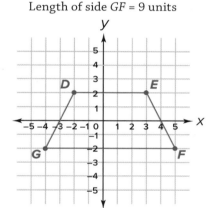

Ace It Time: Peyton graphed a pentagon on the coordinate plane because it is a polygon with five sides, and five vertices.

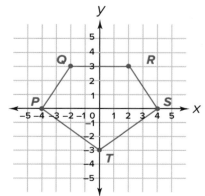

Representing Three-Dimensional Figures Using Nets

Page 148 Practice: Now you try

1. Rectangular prism

2. Cylinder

3. Cube

Page 149

4. Triangular prism (one possible answer):

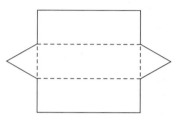

Ace It Time: Kylie is incorrect. All of these nets can be folded into a three-dimensional cube. All eleven nets in the diagram should be circled.

Using Nets to Find Surface Area

Page 150 Practice: Now you try

1. 52 cm²

2. 416 in.²

Page 151

3. 222 cm²

4. 150 cm²

Ace It Time: The surface area of the square pyramid is 85 in.². To find the surface area of the figure, first find the area of each face. The area of the square base is 25 in.² (or 5 in. × 5 in.). The area of each triangle is 15 in.² because $A = \frac{1}{2}bh = \frac{1}{2}(5 \times 6) = 15$. There are 4 triangle faces (15 × 4 = 60). Add them together: 60 in.² + 25 in.² = 85 in.².

Unit 8 Stop and Think! Review

Page 152 Activity Section 1:

1. 56 cm²

2. 10 cm²

3. 21.25 ft²

4. 195 m²

Page 153 Activity Section 2:

1. 480 mm²

2. 128.2 mm²

3. 112 ft²

4. 56 in.²

Activity Section 3:

1. 72 cm³

2. 20 cm³

3. $20\frac{1}{4}$ in.^{3}

4. $299\frac{1}{4}$ ft^3

5. $126\frac{7}{8}$ in.^{3}

6. $4\frac{11}{16}$ ft^3

Page 154 Activity Section 4:

Name the polygon: trapezoid

Explain how you know: There are four sides. The two parallel sides are different lengths.

Length of side DE = 4 units

Length of side GF = 7 units

You can find the length of the sides by counting the distance between each point. You can also use absolute values to find the distance. Add the absolute values of the x-coordinates to find the distance between D and E and the distance between G and F.

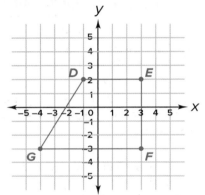

Page 155 Activity Section 5:

1. Cube

2. Triangular prism

3. Triangular prism

4. Pentagonal prism (one possible answer):

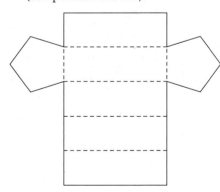

Activity Section 6:

1. 72 cm^2

2. 700 cm^2

3. 432 cm^2

4. 900 in.^{2}

Unit 8 Stop and Think! Understand

Page 156 Activity Section:

The area of the shaded region is 368.5 cm^2. To find this, subtract the area of the unshaded triangle from the shaded parallelogram. The area of the whole parallelogram is

$$A = bh = 23 \times 17 = 391 \text{ cm}^2.$$

The area of the unshaded triangle is

$$A = \frac{1}{2}bh = \frac{1}{2}(9 \times 5) = 22.5 \text{ cm}^2.$$

The total area of the shaded region is

$$391 - 22.5 = 368.5 \text{ cm}^2.$$

Unit 8 Stop and Think! Discover

Page 157 Activity Section:

Darnell will need 360 in.^{2} of paper to cover the box. The amount of paper needed is equal to the surface area. To solve, first draw a net of the triangular prism, including the measurements:

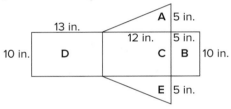

Find the area of each of the faces by using the formula $A = bh$ for the three rectangles and $A = \frac{1}{2}bh$ for the two triangles:

A = 30 in.^{2}

B = 50 in.^{2}

C = 120 in.^{2}

D = 130 in.^{2}

E = 30 in.^{2}

The surface area is the sum of the areas of all the faces:

$$30 + 50 + 120 + 130 + 30 = 360 \text{ in.}^2$$

Unit 9: CORE Statistical Variability Concepts

Recognizing Statistical Questions

Page 158 Practice: Now you try

1. Statistical. The answers will vary because the boys will all be different heights

2. Not statistical. There is only one answer

3. Not statistical. There is only one answer

Page 159

4. Statistical. The answers will vary because Florida does not receive the same amount of rain each June.

5. Not statistical. There is only one answer

6. Statistical. The answers will vary because it can take you different amounts of time to get to school each morning

Ace It Time: This is a statistical question because the answers will vary. Each classmate may spend a different amount of time watching TV each week.

Measures of Center

Page 160 Practice: Now you try

1. Mean: 7; Median: 6; Mode: 6

2. Mean: 30; Median: 30; Mode: 26 and 32

Page 161

3. Mean: 202; Median: 202; Mode: 205

4. Mean: 1,203; Median: 1,203; Mode: 1,203

Ace It Time: Mean: 89; Median; 89.5; Mode: 90

To find the mean of Treyvon's quiz scores, first find the sum of the six scores. Divide the sum by six, which is the total number of data points.

$$85 + 90 + 87 + 93 + 89 + 90 = 534$$
$$534 \div 6 = 89$$

To find the median, list the scores in order from least to greatest

$$85, 87, 89, 90, 90, 93$$

Since two numbers (89 and 90) are in the middle, find their mean.

$$\frac{(89 + 90)}{2} = 89.5$$

The mode is 90 because it is the score that occurs the most often.

Measures of Variation

Page 163 Practice: Now you try

1. Range = 9; IQR = 7

2. Range = 12; IQR = 8

3. Range = 7; IQR = 4

4. Range = 88; IQR = 27

5. Range = 10.5; IQR = 9

6. Range = 850; IQR = 550

Ace It Time: The range is 42 years. The IQR is 6 years.

First, the ages must be ordered from least to greatest:

16, 16, 16, 17, 18, 18, 19, 20, 22, 25, 58

The range is the maximum minus the minimum: 58 − 16 = 42. Don't forget the unit. The measurement is 42 years. The median is 18. It divides the data into two halves.

The lower half: 16, 16, 16, 17, 18. The first quartile is the median, 16.

The upper half: 19, 20, 22, 25, 58. The third quartile is the median, 22.

The IQR is the difference: 22 − 16 = 6 years.

Mean Absolute Deviation

Page 164 Practice: Now you try

1. Mean = 4, MAD = 2
2. Mean = 30, MAD = 16
3. Mean = 250, MAD = 112.5

Page 165

4. Mean = 5.3, MAD = 2.4
5. Mean = 35 miles per hour, MAD = 15 miles per hour
   Explanation: On average, the speed limits vary by 15 miles per hour from the mean. They vary a lot.
6. Mean = 40 years, MAD = 11.25 years
   Explanation: On average, the ages of the teachers vary by 11.25 years from the mean. They vary a lot.

Ace It Time: The mean height of the basketball players is 69 inches. The MAD is 2 inches.

mean height =

$$\frac{65 + 70 + 72 + 68 + 70}{5} = \frac{345}{5} = 69 \text{ in.}$$

Distances from Mean:
(70 appears twice)

$|65 - 69| = |-4| = 4$
$|70 - 69| = |1| = 1$
$|72 - 69| = |3| = 3$
$|68 - 69| = |-1| = 1$

MAD =

$$\frac{4 + 1 + 3 + 1 + 1}{5} = \frac{10}{5} = 2 \text{ in.}$$

The mean height of the gymnasts is 61 inches.

mean height =

$$\frac{60 + 59 + 61 + 63 + 62}{5} = \frac{305}{5} = 61 \text{ in.}$$

Distances from Mean:

$|60 - 61| = |-1| = 1$
$|59 - 61| = |-2| = 2$
$|61 - 61| = |0| = 0$
$|63 - 61| = |2| = 2$
$|62 - 61| = |1| = 1$

MAD =

$$\frac{1 + 2 + 0 + 2 + 1}{5} = \frac{6}{5} = 1.2 \text{ in.}$$

The average height of the basketball players is higher than the gymnasts. This means the basketball players are taller. The MAD of the basketball players is also greater than the gymnasts. This means the basketball players vary more in height. The gymnasts are more similar to each other.

Dot Plots

Page 168 Practice: Now you try

1. Each dot represents the number of texts sent in one day.
2. 9 texts
3. 19.5 texts
4. 19 texts and 20 texts
5. The data clusters around 19 to 20 texts per day. The data is mostly symmetrical.
6. The outlier is 25 texts in one day.
7. Possible dot plot:

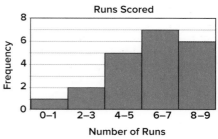

Weights of Packages (lb)

8. The data are not symmetrical but are clustered, with most packages weighing between 17 and 19 pounds.

Page 169

Ace It Time:

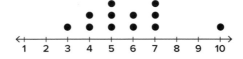

Answers will vary, but the chosen situation should appropriately

represent the data. Statements can include information about the range (7), the median (5.5), the mean (5.75), or the modes (5 and 7). Statements could also describe the clusters at 5 and 7, describe 10 as an outlier, or describe the data as mostly symmetrical.

Histograms

Page 172 Practice: Now you try

1. Sample histogram: Students may use different intervals.

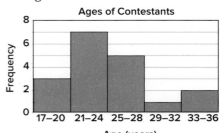

2. The bars are highest on the right. Most of the time, the team scored between 4 and 9 runs.
3. Answer depends on the histogram drawn. For the histogram above, it is 6–7 runs.
4. 18 cats
5. The bars are highest on the left. Most of the cats seen by the veterinarian weigh 15 pounds or less.

Page 173

Ace It Time:

Histogram:

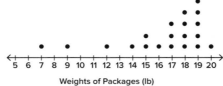

The interval with the highest frequency might contain the mode but it might not. If the 21–24 interval has one data point that happens 7 times, it will be the mode. However, it might have three 22s, three 23s, and one 24. There could be another data point in another interval that happens more than 3 times. There is no way to know for sure where the mode is.

Box Plots

Page 176 Practice: Now you try

1. Box plot:

Ages (in Years) of Used Cars Sold

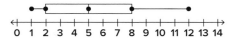

2. Extremes: 1 and 12
   Median: 5
   First and third quartiles: 2 and 8

3. range = 12 – 1 = 11 years

4. IQR = 8 – 2 = 6 years

5. 12 points

6. 25%

7. 50%

Page 177

Ace It Time:
Lower extreme: 64°F
First quartile: 68°F
Median = 72°F
Third quartile: 80°F
Upper extreme: 88°F
Range = 88°F – 64°F = 24°F
IQR = 80°F – 68°F = 12°F

The high temperature ranged from 64°F to 88°F. About half of the time, the temperature ranged from 68°F to 80°F.

Choosing Measures to Describe Data

Page 179 Practice: Now you try

1. The median is the best measure of center. There are two outliers at 2 and 5 that will change the mean. The median will describe the center of most of the data.

2. The IQR is the better measure of spread. Since IQR measures the middle of the data, it won't include the outliers. This means it will describe the spread of most of the data.

Ace It Time: Answers will vary, but students should recognize that it's not impossible to use MAD to describe the data. They should argue their point.

Jamie says you cannot use MAD, which means it is a bad measurement. This is incorrect. You can use MAD to describe the data, although some people might

use another measurement. There are symmetrical clusters in the data. You can point to the middle, where a lot of the data points are. The mean could be a good measure of center. This means you can use the MAD, since you use the mean to find it.

However, mean and MAD are not the only good measures. You can also use median. Since most of the data is toward the middle of the plot, IQR might be a good measure.

Unit 9 Stop and Think! Review

Page 180 Activity Section 1:

1. A

2. B

3. A statistical question has many possible answers. A non-statistical question only has one answer.

Activity Section 2:

1. Mean = $27; Mode = $25

2. Mean = 23 seconds; Median = 22.6 seconds; Mode = 22.6 seconds

Page 181 Activity Section 3:

1. Range = 11°F; IQR = 8°F.

2. Range = 18 minutes; IQR = 10 minutes.

Activity Section 4:

1. Mean = 146; MAD = 11.2

2. Mean = 57; MAD = 5

Page 182 Activity Section 5:

1. 20 classmates

2. 6 books

3. 5 books

4. 5.5 books

5. 5 books

6. The number of books peaks at 5. The data is mostly symmetrical.

Activity Section 6:

1. 120 phone calls

2. 18–23 minutes

3. 25 phone calls

4. 75 phone calls

5. You can't tell what the median is from a histogram.

Page 183 Activity Section 7:

1. 16 pounds

2. 9 pounds

3. 8 pounds

Activity Section 8:

Sample Answers:

1. Most of the data are clustered together, but it is not totally symmetrical. There are two outliers at 15 texts per day. Outliers affect the mean.

2. The median is a better measure of center because it cannot be affected by the outliers.

3. The IQR is a better measure of variation because it is not affected by the outliers. The IQR shows the middle 50% of the data, so it is a better measure.

Page 184

4. The data are clustered at both ends, with a space in the middle. It is mostly symmetrical. It does not affect the mean. Since there is a gap right in the middle, the median might not represent the center. The median will be in one of the clusters of data.

5. The mean is a better measure of center because it is the average of all of the data values. It is not affected by the gap in the center.

6. The range and MAD are both good measures of variation. The IQR is not a good choice because it represents the middle of the data, where there is a gap.

Unit 9 Stop and Think! Understand

Page 185 Activity Section:

The range is 67 people.
The median is 139.5 people.
The IQR is 37 people.
The mean is 134 people.
The MAD is 19 people.

Unit 9 Stop and Think! Discover

Page 186 Activity Section:

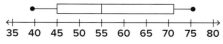

Median = 55
Lower quartile = 45
Upper quartile = 72
IQR = 27

Tape Diagrams

10%	20%	30%	40%	50%	60%	70%	80%	90%	100%

10%	20%	30%	40%	50%	60%	70%	80%	90%	100%

10%	20%	30%	40%	50%	60%	70%	80%	90%	100%

10%	20%	30%	40%	50%	60%	70%	80%	90%	100%

10%	20%	30%	40%	50%	60%	70%	80%	90%	100%

10%	20%	30%	40%	50%	60%	70%	80%	90%	100%

10%	20%	30%	40%	50%	60%	70%	80%	90%	100%

Number Lines

Coordinate Planes

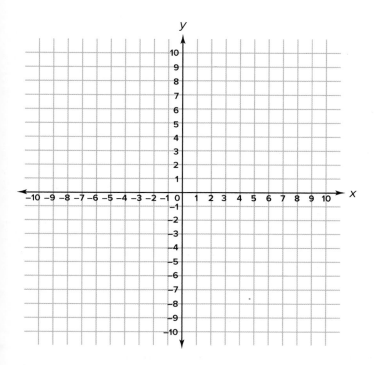

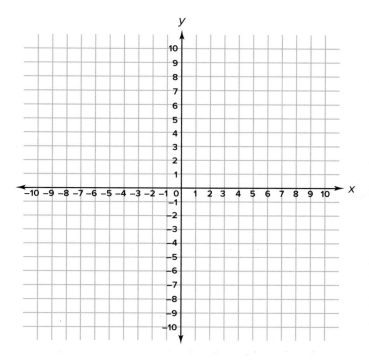

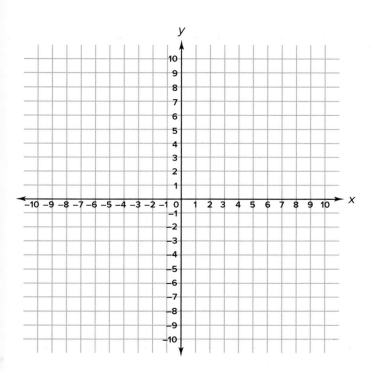

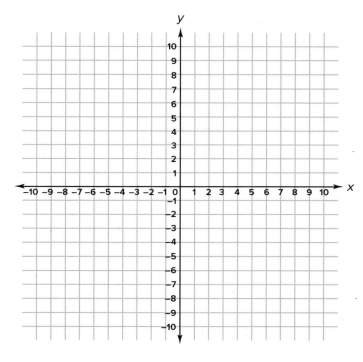

Grid Paper

Measurement Charts

Customary Units Charts

Length
12 in. = 1 ft
3 ft = 1 yd
5,280 ft = 1 mi
1,760 yd = 1 mi

Weight
16 oz = 1 lb
1 ton = 2,000 lb

Capacity
128 fl. oz = 1 gal
2 pt = 1 qt
8 pt = 1 gal
4 qt = 1 gal

Time
60 sec = 1 min
60 min = 1 hr
24 hr = 1 day
7 days = 1 wk
52 wk = 1 yr
12 mon = 1 yr
365 days = 1 yr

Metric Units Charts

Length
1 km = 1,000 m
1 m = .001 km
1 m = 100 cm
1 m = 1,000 mm
1 mm = .001 m

Weight
1 kg = 1,000 g
1 g = .001 kg
1 g = 100 cg
1 cg = .01 g
1 mg = .001 g

Capacity
1 kL = 1,000 L
1 L = .001 kL
1 L = 100 cL
1 cL = .01 L
1 L = 1,000 mL
1 mL = .001 L

Area Formulas

triangles

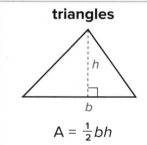

$$A = \tfrac{1}{2}bh$$

parallelograms

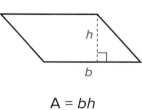

$$A = bh$$

trapezoids

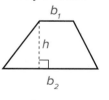

$$A = \tfrac{1}{2}(b_1 + b_2)h$$

Volume Formula

$V = l \times w \times h$

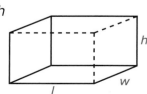

$V = Bh$

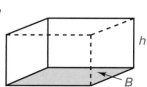

GRADES 2–6
TEST PRACTICE
for Common Core

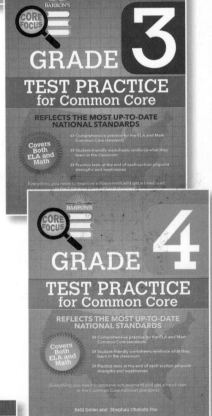

With Common Core Standards being implemented across America, it's important to give students, teachers, and parents the tools they need to achieve success. That's why Barron's has created the *Core Focus* series. These multi-faceted, grade-specific workbooks are designed for self-study learning, and the units in each book are divided into thematic lessons that include:

- Specific, focused practice through a variety of exercises, including multiple-choice, short answer, and extended response questions
- A unique scaffolded layout that organizes questions in a way that challenges students to apply the standards in multiple formats
- "Fast Fact" boxes and a cumulative assessment in Mathematics and English Language Arts (ELA) to help students increase knowledge and demonstrate understanding across the standards

Perfect for in-school or at-home study, these engaging and versatile workbooks will help students meet and exceed the expectations of the Common Core.

Grade 2 Test Practice for Common Core
Maryrose Walsh and Judith Brendel
ISBN 978-1-4380-0550-8
Paperback, $14.99, *Can$16.99*

Grade 3 Test Practice for Common Core
Renee Snyder, M.A. and Susan M. Signet, M.A.
ISBN 978-1-4380-0551-5
Paperback, $14.99, *Can$16.99*

Grade 4 Test Practice for Common Core
Kelli Dolan and Shephali Chokshi-Fox
ISBN 978-1-4380-0515-7
Paperback, $14.99, *Can$16.99*

Grade 5 Test Practice for Common Core
Lisa M. Hall and Sheila Frye
ISBN 978-1-4380-0595-9
Paperback, $14.99, *Can$16.99*

Grade 6 Test Practice for Common Core
Christine R. Gray and Carrie Meyers-Herron
ISBN 978-1-4380-0592-8
Paperback, $14.99, *Can$16.99*

Barron's Educational Series, Inc.
250 Wireless Blvd.
Hauppauge, N.Y. 11788
Order toll-free: 1-800-645-3476

In Canada:
Georgetown Book Warehouse
34 Armstrong Ave.
Georgetown, Ontario L7G 4R9
Canadian orders: 1-800-247-7160

Prices subject to change without notice.

Coming soon to your local book store or visit **www.barronseduc.com**

(#295 R11/14)